Kindle Fire

the missing manual®

The book that should have been in the box®

Peter Meyers

O'REILLY®

Beijing | Cambridge | Farnham | Köln | Sebastopol | Tokyo

Kindle Fire: The Missing Manual
By Peter Meyers

Published by O'Reilly Media, Inc., 1005 Gravenstein Highway North,
Sebastopol, CA 95472.

O'Reilly books may be purchased for educational, business, or sales promotional use. Online editions are also available for most titles (*http://my.safaribooksonline .com*). For more information, contact our corporate/institutional sales department: 800.998.9938 or *corporate@oreilly.com*.

Editor: Nan Barber
Production Editor: Holly Bauer
Proofreader: Carla Spoon
Illustrations: Rob Romano and Rebecca Demarest

Indexer: Ron Strauss
Cover Designers: Randy Comer, Karen Montgomery, and Suzy Wiviott
Interior Designers: Ron Bilodeau and J.D. Biersdorfer

February 2012:   First Edition.

Revision History for the First Edition:

2012-02-02   First release

See *http://oreilly.com/catalog/errata.csp?isbn=9781449316273* for release details.

ISBN: 978-1-449-31627-3
[TI]

Contents

PART I   **Getting Started and Reading**

CHAPTER 1

CHAPTER 2

CHAPTER 3

PART V **Appendixes**

The Missing Credits

About the Author

Peter Meyers designs, speaks, and writes about digital books. For more than two decades, he's worked at the intersection of writing and technology. He cofounded Digital Learning Interactive, a pioneering multimedia textbook publisher (sold in 2004 to Thomson Learning). Peter has also written about the strange and wonderful effects of computers on mainstream culture for many publications, including the *New York Times*, the *Wall Street Journal*, *Wired*, *Salon*, and the *Village Voice*. During a five-year tour of duty at O'Reilly Media he worked in the Missing Manual group, serving as managing editor and associate publisher. He's also the author of *Best iPad Apps* and *Breaking the Page: Transforming Books and the Reading Experience*. Peter's undergraduate degree is from Harvard, where he studied American history and literature, and he has an MFA in fiction from the Iowa Writers' Workshop. He lives with his wife and two daughters in "upstate Manhattan" (aka Washington Heights). Online, you can find his blog at *http://newkindofbook.com* and his tweets at *http://twitter.com/petermeyers*.

About the Creative Team

Nan Barber (editor) has been working with the Missing Manual series since its inception. She lives in Massachusetts with her husband, a variety of electronic gadgets, and a stack of dictionaries. Email: *nanbarber@oreilly.com*.

Holly Bauer (production editor) resides in Ye Olde Cambridge, MA. She's a production editor by day and an avid home cook, prolific DIYer, and mid-century modern furniture enthusiast by night/weekend. Email: *holly@oreilly.com*.

Carla Spoon (proofreader) is a freelance writer and copy editor. An avid runner, she works and feeds her tech gadget addiction from her home office in the shadow of Mount Rainier. Email: *carla_spoon@comcast.net*.

Ron Strauss (indexer) specializes in the indexing of information technology publications of all kinds. Ron is also an accomplished classical violist and lives in northern California with his wife and fellow indexer, Annie, and his miniature pinscher, Kanga. Email: *rstrauss@mchsi.com*.

Rachel Roumeliotis (technical reviewer) is an editor at O'Reilly Media, Inc. She has been a bibliophile for as long as she can remember and is very interested in seeing where the book business is going and how she can be a part of it. She has too many books both on her shelves and in her Kindles. Email: *rroumeliotis@oreilly.com*.

Acknowledgments

The Missing Manual series doesn't accept ads, but I can't resist kicking these thanks off with an uncompensated word of gratitude to the makers of Cafe du Monde. Friends, this is some writing-friendly coffee! In the department of humans that helped, Brian Sawyer gave me the green light on this project and to him I am grateful. At Amazon, both Kevin Molloy and Leslie Letts were patient, valuable guides to the Fire. They answered many questions that I would have had to spend hours hunting down on my own. On a related note, technical reviewer Rachel Roumeliotis did a thorough job of spotting missing or confusing explanations. Indexer Ron Strauss put together the subject finder at the back of this book; as a huge fan of that overlooked art, I wanted to say thanks for doing such a great job on that front. What this book contains, of course, is more than just words, and for the finely polished images and labels I wanted to tip my hat to an old pal, Rob Romano. Equally important is Holly Bauer's work; each page layout is a beautifully crafted combo of words and pictures thanks to her fine interior design skills. Speaking of prose: My editor Nan Barber has demonstrated why she belongs in the Missing Manual Hall of Fame; thanks to her, with ample help from proofreader Carla Spoon, lots o' flab and fuzzy verbiage got trimmed and clarified.

On the home front, this writing project couldn't have happened if not for the help of various NYC-based SilverMeyers who pitched in on the babysitting front. My Mom and Dad, my sister Jen, Aunt Madge, and Grandma and Grandpa Silverman: Thanks to you all for freeing me up to stay in my writing cave. To my girls Willa and Esme: Thank you for giving me the incentive every day to write faster. You wee tots will always be more entertaining than any gadget. And, Ms. Esme, I hope I have succeeded in eliminating enough "boring" words to make this book interesting—that's a tough one! Finally, to Lisa, for giving up almost a full season's worth of weekends, for supporting her guy's gadget jones, and for making it possible for me to do what I love: Thank you; you are the real fire in my life.

—Peter Meyers

The Missing Manual Series

Missing Manuals are witty, superbly written guides to computer products that don't come with printed manuals (which is just about all of them). Each book features a handcrafted index and cross-references to specific pages (not just chapters). Recent and upcoming titles include:

Access 2010: The Missing Manual by Matthew MacDonald

Buying a Home: The Missing Manual by Nancy Conner

CSS: The Missing Manual, Second Edition, by David Sawyer McFarland

Creating a Website: The Missing Manual, Third Edition, by Matthew MacDonald

David Pogue's Digital Photography: The Missing Manual by David Pogue

Dreamweaver CS5.5: The Missing Manual by David Sawyer McFarland

Droid 2: The Missing Manual by Preston Gralla

Droid X2: The Missing Manual by Preston Gralla

Excel 2010: The Missing Manual by Matthew MacDonald

Facebook: The Missing Manual, Third Edition by E.A. Vander Veer

FileMaker Pro 11: The Missing Manual by Susan Prosser and Stuart Gripman

Flash CS5.5: The Missing Manual by Chris Grover

Galaxy S II: The Missing Manual by Preston Gralla

Galaxy Tab: The Missing Manual by Preston Gralla

Google+: The Missing Manual by Kevin Purdy

Google Apps: The Missing Manual by Nancy Conner

Google SketchUp: The Missing Manual by Chris Grover

HTML5: The Missing Manual by Matthew MacDonald

iMovie '11 & iDVD: The Missing Manual by David Pogue and Aaron Miller

iPad 2: The Missing Manual, Third Edition by J.D. Biersdorfer

iPhone: The Missing Manual, Fifth Edition by David Pogue

iPhone App Development: The Missing Manual by Craig Hockenberry

iPhoto '11: The Missing Manual by David Pogue and Lesa Snider

iPod: The Missing Manual, Tenth Edition by J.D. Biersdorfer and David Pogue

JavaScript & jQuery: The Missing Manual, Second Edition by David Sawyer McFarland

Living Green: The Missing Manual by Nancy Conner

Mac OS X Lion: The Missing Manual by David Pogue

Mac OS X Snow Leopard: The Missing Manual by David Pogue

Microsoft Project 2010: The Missing Manual by Bonnie Biafore

Motorola Xoom: The Missing Manual by Preston Gralla

Netbooks: The Missing Manual by J.D. Biersdorfer

NOOK Tablet: The Missing Manual by Preston Gralla

Office 2010: The Missing Manual by Nancy Connor, Chris Grover, and Matthew MacDonald

Office 2011 for Macintosh: The Missing Manual by Chris Grover

Palm Pre: The Missing Manual by Ed Baig

Personal Investing: The Missing Manual by Bonnie Biafore

Photoshop CS5: The Missing Manual by Lesa Snider

Photoshop Elements 10: The Missing Manual by Barbara Brundage

PHP & MySQL: The Missing Manual by Brett McLaughlin

PowerPoint 2007: The Missing Manual by E.A. Vander Veer

Premiere Elements 8: The Missing Manual by Chris Grover

QuickBase: The Missing Manual by Nancy Conner

QuickBooks 2012: The Missing Manual by Bonnie Biafore

Quicken 2009: The Missing Manual by Bonnie Biafore

Switching to the Mac: The Missing Manual, Lion Edition by David Pogue

Wikipedia: The Missing Manual by John Broughton

Windows Vista: The Missing Manual by David Pogue

Windows 7: The Missing Manual by David Pogue

Word 2007: The Missing Manual by Chris Grover

Your Body: The Missing Manual by Matthew MacDonald

Your Brain: The Missing Manual by Matthew MacDonald

Your Money: The Missing Manual by J.D. Roth

For a full list of all Missing Manuals in print, go to *www.missingmanuals.com/ library.html*.

Introduction

WHY IS THE KINDLE Fire such a big deal? After all, Samsung, Motorola, HP—the list goes on—have built iPad wannabes...that most shoppers ignored. Amazon's stroke of genius was deciding not to go head-to-head against Apple. Instead, they built a tablet that was vastly more affordable, much smaller, and still does what most folks want: email, ebooks, the Web, videos, and apps.

Less than two months after the Fire's release, Amazon shared the early results. Of the many, many items it sells, the Fire had become the bestselling, most gifted, and most wished-for product. Congratulations, then, on having picked a leader in the Great Tablet Derby of the 2010s.

The Fire is deceptively powerful. Though it's got only a few physical buttons, underneath its sleek, simple exterior lies a machine that can do as much as a "real" computer. It's a Kindle so, of course, you can buy and read ebooks. But because it's a multi-purpose tablet, that's just one of its many talents. With it, you also get:

- **TV set and movie screen.** Bring a Fire into bed or onto the bus, and you've got your own personal entertainment center. Amazon's Hollywood and TV studio dealmakers have put together a cheap and large catalog that's big enough to rival Netflix and iTunes. Your choices, of course, are smaller than what you'd find on a normal boob tube or cineplex, but you still have thousands and thousands of titles to pick from. This particular revolution is just getting started and it's wickedly fun for any moving image fan.

- **Web browser.** Most phones nowadays give you some way to surf. But even the biggest smartest phone is still around the size of your palm. The Fire's extra real estate really helps you appreciate the Web. What you see on its shiny, multi-million colored display is pretty near close to what you see on a full-size computer. The Fire can also play multimedia Flash content (videos, games, and, yes, ads)—a checkbox that the iPad will never tick off.

- **Email, chat, and social networking.** It's all here. However you connect, the Fire is ready to help. It has a nifty built-in email program and lets you install your choice of third-party apps for Facebook, Twitter, and more.

- **Portable picture frame.** TV, movies, and the Web aren't always enough. Sometimes the best home entertainment is the kind you make with your own family: pet photos, vacation albums, and birthday party and camping videos. If you can capture it on a digital camera or camcorder, you can show it off on the Fire. Photo sharing in particular is a blast. No longer do your friends have to squint at the cellphone screen to watch little Eddie make the diving catch. The Fire's big enough to really light up people's faces.

- **Digital briefcase.** Tired of fumbling around with printouts? With the Fire, you never have to bother printing hotel confirmations, online shopping receipts, or the work documents you want to read on the train. Out of the box, the Fire is ready to display any Microsoft Word or PDF file. A few add-on apps, which you'll meet in Chapter 4, extend that list to almost any document type you've ever heard of.

- **Jukebox.** Amazon's been hard at work stocking the shelves of its digital record shop. Even better, it's designed free software that makes it easy to remain a loyal Apple fan while playing its tunes on non-iGadgets—the Fire very much included. Whether you plug in a pair of earphones, play your music aloud on the Fire's built-in speakers, or connect a pair of legit speakers, this gadget's great for tuning in and turning on.

- **Video game player.** Angry Birds, Fruit Ninja, even 21st-century versions of Pac Man and Pong—it's all here on the Fire, plus a cool 5,000 or so other options. A quick list of key categories include: race car driving; football, soccer, and pool; word and number puzzles; card games; pinball; and strategy and adventure fests. Hardcore teenage gamers may need a dedicated gadget for high-end performance, but for the rest of us, the Fire is a pretty amazing portable arcade.

- **Everything else.** Speaking of apps: Anything the Fire can't do out of the box, some developer somewhere is probably working on. Weather report videos, podcasts and worldwide radio tuners, recipe displays, sleep-inducing white noise machines, horoscope advisors, family calendar keepers. These are just a few of the apps that are *currently* available on the Fire. About half of these special-purpose programs are free, and most cost no more than a buck or two.

TIP One simple way to load up on apps is via Amazon's daily giveaway. At the very top of the Appstore (either on your Fire or on Amazon.com), a paid app's price gets slashed to the low, low price of free. Page 28 has details on downloading and other app suggestions. Also check out the final three chapters of this book, which are dedicated to guiding you through the many app options that await.

Under the Fire's Hood

Making all this happen is a combination of hardware and software that matches the Fire's exterior: simple and sufficient to get the job done. Weighing in at 14.6 ounces, the Fire packs 8 GB of storage (only about 6 GB is available for your use; the rest is occupied by the system and other built-in software). That's enough to hold about 80 apps, plus some combination of 10 movies, 800 songs, or 6,000 books. The screen is a 16-million-color IPS display. That's short for *in-plane switching*, which means that even if you're not looking directly at the Fire, what's on screen still looks clear. In other words: two kids in the back seat of a car both get a decent view of the movie. A full charge of the non-removable battery gets you about 8 hours of use.

Most significant is the underlying software. You may have heard that the Fire uses the Google-designed and freely available Android operating system. (Version number 2.3, nicknamed Gingerbread, for those keeping score at home.) But you'd never know it if you compared the Fire to one of the other Android-powered tablets out there—Amazon made all sorts of custom changes. You'll read about the details in the pages ahead, but in effect, Amazon laid an easy-to-operate topcoat of its own design over the basic Android framework. Aside from the fact that Amazon gets its base layer of programming for free, the other beneficiary is you, given that many Android apps are playable on the Fire.

NOTE This book covers version number 6.2.1 of the Fire's system software. If Amazon's past history with the other Kindle devices is any indication, the company will push out new updates with bug fixes and feature additions every couple of months.

About This Book

Tucked alongside the Fire and its power cord is a playing card–sized "getting to know your Kindle" guide. It's enough to usher you onto the home screen, where you'll find a bare-bones User's Guide—the kind that covers a headline-only list of features, without telling you much about which ones are most worth your time. This Missing Manual, then, is the book that should have come in the box. In the pages ahead, you'll learn about all the Fire's nooks and crannies. But what's more valuable, you'll find out which apps and options work best and which items are still works in progress. You'll also get real-world counsel on how to beef up the Fire's still-developing talents with third-party apps.

About the Outline

The book is divided into five parts, each containing a handful of chapters. Everything's arranged to help you get the most out of the Fire's key talents, from reading and watching to staying in touch and using apps. You'll find it helpful to start with Chapter 1 for a quick tour of the Fire's parts and navigation. After that, read the chapters in any order you like—page-specific cross references point you to related material you'll need to understand any explanation. What follows is a highlight reel of what each part contains:

- **Part I, Getting Started and Reading.** The first chapter explains what you need to know about how the Fire organizes its contents and how to operate its touchscreen controls. *Reading Books* (Chapter 2) tells the story of every Kindle's main talent; it's also where audio books are covered. *The Newsstand* (Chapter 3) is next, with coverage on finding, buying, and reading magazines and newspapers (both plain-text editions and multimedia-powered app versions). *Documents and Spreadsheets* (Chapter 4) is primarily for Microsoft Office fans—be they businesspeople or students—but it's also where you'll learn how to do things like read PDF files and load the Fire with ebooks that don't come from Amazon.

- **Part II, Watching and Listening.** That beautiful screen you're holding is ready to show off beautiful images—moving and still alike. *Watching TV and Movies* (Chapter 5) introduces you to the ever-growing commercial lineup that Amazon offers, ready for display not just on the Fire, but also on your computer and network-ready TV. For your own version of showtime, *Photos and Home Videos* (Chapter 6) gives you the scoop on getting your own pictures and movies onto the small screen. *Listening to Music* (Chapter 7) is more than just about buying and playing the 18 million songs Amazon now sells. You'll also find out how to import any existing iTunes or Windows Media Player collections you have, as well as the kinds of apps you'll need to play podcasts and even real radio.

- **Part III, Communications and Browsing.** The Fire's WiFi connection is ready to do more, of course, than just buy books and songs and movies. *Email and Address Book* (Chapter 8) explains how to get the most out of two apps that ship with the Fire and *Browsing the Web* (Chapter 9) sets you up with Silk, Amazon's homemade Internet explorer.

- **Part IV, Kindle in Appland.** The hundreds of thousands of special purpose programs—apps, as they're commonly called—that have revolutionized the software industry and filled our virtual skies with Angry Birds are available, or coming soon, to your Fire. Amazon's set up a special store (the Appstore for Android) where it vets each submission to make sure it's Fire-compatible. The chapters here—*Playing Games* (Chapter 10), *Creative Corner* (Chapter 11), and *Managing Time, Tasks, and Travel* (Chapter 12)—distinguish the best from the rest, in an effort to help you spend your app budget wisely.

- **Part V, Appendices.** Two brief, back-of-the-book help guides. The first (*Settings* [Appendix A]) guides you through every option in the buried-deep control room of that same name. The second (*Troubleshooting and Maintenance* [Appendix B]) lays out a half dozen or so remedies to the most common Fire ailments and lists links to some helpful advice and support sites.

About→These→Arrows

In order to keep the navigational pointers in this, as well as every Missing Manual, concise, we've adopted a simple shorthand for pointing out how to burrow through menu or button hierarchies. Rather than slowing you down with a cumbersome series of instructions—*Tap the middle of the screen to summon the Options bar; on it, tap the Menu button and, from the row that pops up above it, touch Now Playing*—a series of arrows helps more efficiently convey that info, like so: Options bar→Menu→Now Playing.

About MissingManuals.com

This book is loaded with web links. If you're reading the print edition, sure, you can type in each address every time you want to visit an online pointer. Why not, though, bookmark the Missing CD page for this title (*www.missingmanuals.com/cds/firemm*)? There you'll find a list of every link mentioned within these pages.

The Missing CD page also offers corrections and updates to the book. To see them, click the View Errata link. You're invited to submit corrections and updates yourself by clicking "Submit your own errata" on the same page. To keep this book as up to date and accurate as possible, each time we print more copies, we'll make any confirmed corrections you've suggested. Or go directly to the errata page at *www.tinyurl.com/fire-mm*.

While you're online, you can register this book at *http://oreilly.com/register*. Registering means we can send you updates about the book, and you'll be eligible for special offers like discounts on future editions of *Kindle Fire: The Missing Manual*.

Safari Books Online

Safari® Books Online is an on-demand digital library that lets you search over 7,500 technology books and videos.

With a subscription, you can read any page and watch any video from our library. Access new titles before they're available in print. Copy and paste code samples, organize your favorites, download chapters, bookmark key sections, create notes, print out pages, and benefit from tons of other time-saving features.

O'Reilly Media has uploaded this book to the Safari Books Online service. To have full digital access to this book and others on similar topics from O'Reilly and other publishers, sign up for free at *http://my.safaribooksonline.com*.

Getting Started and Reading

CHAPTER 1

Out of the Box: Setting Up, Taking a Tour

DID YOU KNOW THAT serious gadget geeks treat device openings as YouTube-worthy rituals? They actually videotape, narrate (*my hand is shaking from the fatigue of waiting in line all night...*), and then post the entire experience online—from waiting in line to opening the package to a tour of the interface. Assuming your day job leaves you little time for YouTube, consider this chapter your own Kindle Fire meet 'n' greet.

When you first unpack the Fire, you'll notice that Amazon has kept physical buttons and ports to a bare minimum. It's *inside*, once you've flipped Fire on, that might take a little getting used to. Here, you'll encounter a navigational system for programs and files that looks absolutely nothing like what you've seen on a regular computer. Instead, think super-sized smartphone or souped-up ATM.

In the following pages, you'll learn much more than simply how to turn the Fire on and enter your account info. You'll see how to control the device using neither mouse nor menu. You'll get touchscreen basics, including some taps and tricks that will make your time in TouchLand more enjoyable. Finally, you'll take a trip into the Cloud for a brief but necessary introduction to how Amazon expects anyone with a sizable digital media collection to enjoy it all given the Fire's small storage saddles. Fasten your seat belt—videotaping what lies ahead is strictly optional.

Parts and Ports

Amazon has made a serious commitment to minimalist hardware design—no small feat for a firm whose first device, the original Kindle, had more buttons than a tailor's shop. There's the 7-inch screen, of course; a black border and rubberized backside for gripping the gadget; and a mere five buttons, openings, and exits:

- **Combo charging and USB port.** On the bottom of the device is where you insert the one and only accessory that comes in the box—the power cord. Should you wish to transfer digital files directly from a Mac or PC to the Fire (a strictly optional maneuver covered in detail starting on page 77), you can stick a USB cable here. If you're like most people, most of the time, you'll use this port for battery refills.

- **On/off switch.** This nubbin, right next to the power port, is about as big as a candy dot. In addition to letting you turn the Fire on and off, it's also how you put it to sleep (a power-saving mode that's quicker to rejuvenate than a cold start).

TIP A common criticism of this first Fire is the placement of its power button. Down there on the bottom of the device, it's *way* too easy to hit accidentally, say the complainers. If you agree, here's a simple fix: rotate the Fire 180 degrees. What's onscreen shifts to match how your Fire is oriented, and the offending button is on top, safely away from unintentional turnoffs.

- **Audio port.** Stick pretty much any gadget-friendly headphone in this 3.5-millimeter opening; the sounds that ensue will be for your ears only.

- **Speakers.** When headphone-free, the Fire plays its beats and beeps through this extremely modest pair of top-mounted stereo speakers.

NOTE   Want to connect external speakers? No problem. They'll need their own power source (like most any that work with an iPod or computer) and have that toothpick-sized 3.5-millimeter plug.

Turning the Fire On, Making It Yours

If by some miracle of self-restraint you haven't turned the Fire on, do so now by pressing the power button. Holding the button for a second is plenty long enough to do the trick. The device logo greets you, followed by a screen sporting some time zone's version of now. Any finger will do as your entry key: Swipe the big orange arrow from right to left. You've arrived at the "Welcome to Kindle Fire" screen.

As you probably know, the Fire connects to the world at large via WiFi. (See the box on page 16 for a WiFi primer.) Ahead, you'll learn about plenty you can do when *not* in range of one of these wireless Internet zones. But the setup process and all your initial Fire fiddling are much simpler when you're in a hotspot. Once you're appropriately situated, your first steps are pretty straightforward:

If WiFi is truly nowhere to be found (perhaps you're unboxing on a plane), tap the link that says "Complete setup later" and then dismiss the message warning you about all the fun you're missing out on—ebook and music buying, app downloading, and so on. When you do get within WiFi range, you need to take care of two chores: Connect to a WiFi network and register your Fire with Amazon. The Quick Settings menu (page 22) is where you make both happen.

❶ **Connect to a WiFi network.** A list of available hotspots appears, with tiny lock icons next to any that require a password. Tap the name of the one you wish to log into. Apartment dwellers may need to scroll down to see the full list. (Scrolling instructions await on page 25 for touchscreen rookies. The short version: Place and hold you finger on the screen and then drag up or down in the direction you want the list to move.) If you're seeing one of those locks, and you've been given the password, enter it on the screen that appears after you tap the network's name.

WiFi 101

WiFi is the only way for the Fire to browse the Web, download apps, and do email. If you don't have much experience in the ways of WiFi (what, you don't already have your own home WiFi network?), here are some basics that'll help you get—and stay—connected.

- **Network SSID.** Geek-speak for a WiFi network's name. On the Fire, you see this term only if you burrow deep down on the "Connect to a network" list and tap "Add a Network" to manually enter a network's name, as described in the Note following Step 1 on page 17. Some restaurants and libraries use this term, so now you know how to translate it into plain English.

- **Security.** For reasons roughly similar to why front doors come with locks, most people secure the WiFi networks they set up. That way, anyone who wants to log on needs to enter a password. Over the past decade or so, a bunch of more or less incompatible security methods have gained varying degrees of popularity. When you encounter a protected network, your Fire asks you to enter a password. In most cases that's all you need to do. (If you're following the Note on page 17, also pick the protocol flavor matching the WiFi network you're connecting to. Fire is conversant in all the popular varieties, from oldest and least secure [WEP] to the more modern and harder-to-hack WPA. The latter comes in four flavors, all of which you find in the Add Network's Security pull-down menu: WPA PSK, WPA2 PSK, WPA EAP, WPA2 EAP.)

- **Channels.** WiFi radio waves make their journey between Internet router and device using one of a dozen or so different channels. Most civilians never have any reason to pick one of these numbers manually (which range from 1 to 14) since the coordination usually happens automatically. The receiving device (like the Fire) picks up whichever channel the broadcaster (the router) uses. In Europe and Japan, channels 12, 13, and 14 are more frequently used than channels 1 and 6, which are common in North American WiFi exchanges. If you travel to either of these regions and find you're having trouble connecting, head to Quick Settings→WiFi→AdvancedSettings→Enable International Channels and pick either "Europe - Channels 12 and 13" or "Japan - Channels 12, 13 and 14" to help tune in.

- **Finding a WiFi network.** Starbucks, McDonald's, and your local public library are all good places to start. Many of these establishments offer free WiFi, asking only that you first visit a web page and agree to some reasonable rules (*I will not download the entire Internet or broadcast naughty images*). On the Fire, the typical sequence goes like this: Go to Quick Settings→WiFi and tap whatever network name the help desk or cashier tells you to look for. In the dialog box that springs up, choose Connect. If the WiFi provider wants you to agree to some good behavior terms, you'll see another box asking if you wish to sign in; tap OK. Then there's the page of legalese, which typically requires you to turn on a checkbox and then tap a button to continue. Finally, tap the upper-right Close button, and you're free to roam around the Internet.

Some security-conscious citizens hide their WiFi network's name from publicly viewable lists, like the one you see on page 15. If that describes you (or, more likely, your teenage WiFi administrator), scroll to the bottom of the list, tap "Enter other Wi-Fi network," type your network's name (in the box that says Network SSID), pick the security method from the drop-down menu of that name, and then enter a password.

❷ **Pick a time zone.** Tap to choose from the list of U.S. options, or pick from a list of worldwide alternatives by opening the "Select another time zone" menu. Then hit Continue.

TIP When you see one of those tappable empty circles (web designers call 'em *radio buttons*), you don't have to tap precisely on the button. Anywhere on the row where it's located will do just fine.

❸ **Register your Kindle.** If you bought it yourself—that is, using your own Amazon account—the Fire has your account info already filled in, as you'll see on the next screen, which greets you by name. If someone else purchased it for you, as a gift, say, tap *Not Donald Trump* and then log in using your own Amazon account. (Don't have one? The box on page 19 shows you how to knock out that must-do chore.) Finally, tap the Get Started Now button.

If a software update is available—a likely occurrence in these early days of bug-squashing and feature-adding—the Fire will immediately start downloading it. Though the Fire offers you an option to pause this operation and resume later, it's best to incorporate these changes as Amazon issues them. After digesting the new software the device shuts down; restart it by pressing the power button to pick up again from this point.

❹ **Take a whirl through the quick start tips Amazon has scrawled on your screen.** Sure, you've got this book, but you have no choice but to tap through each of the mini-tutorial's Next buttons (in the lower-right corner) before you can start using the Fire. Tap Close on the last screen when you're done. Now you're on the home screen.

Rotation and Orientation

Sometimes you want to hold the Fire upright, like a paperback. Sometimes you want to turn it on its side for race-car driving or movie watching. The first is often referred to as *portrait mode* (think Mona Lisa); the sideways pivot is called *landscape* (think, well, a nice wide landscape). Like any modern touchscreen device, the Fire is smart enough to sense when you switch. It reorients whatever is onscreen to match the mode you're in. Try it now to experience one of a new tablet owner's small but delightful pleasures.

NOTE Most apps (for ebook reading, browsing the web, and so on) will shift their contents according to how you're holding the Fire. Sometimes, however, a no-shift order has been programmed in by an app developer. In the Fire's own video-watching app, for example, you can hold the device in portrait mode but the show remains in landscape. Makes sense, if you think about it, considering how truncated things would look if a movie got crammed into the narrow width of portrait mode.

UP TO SPEED

Creating an Amazon Account

Amazon says it's got more than 150 million registered customers. But that still leaves a few folks who've never entered this virtual store. If you're among them, here's how to gain access to all the shopportunities (including plenty of free samples) that await. Using any web browser, surf over to *www.amazon.com* and, at the top of the screen, click the "Start here" link. (You can, of course, use the Fire's browser; tap the Web link on the top of the home screen. Head over to Chapter 9 if you need help steering that software.)

On the page that appears, enter an email address and turn on the radio button that says "No, I am a new customer." Then click the yellow "Sign in..." button. On the next screen, fill in your name, create a password, and then click "Create account." Amazon gives you a bunch of ways to personalize what you see in its aisles—by asking you to give a thumbs up to a bunch of products it parades in front of you. That process, amusingly called the Amazon Betterizer, is completely optional.

Turning the Fire Off

The party's barely started, but perhaps you need a break from all this gadget-induced excitement. You have two alternatives: powering the Fire down and putting it to sleep. What's the difference? The first saves more battery life, but requires more time to power back on (about 30 seconds, versus pretty much instantaneously to wake from sleeping). The choice, of course, is yours, but plenty of people rarely turn their Fires off completely.

To power down completely, press and hold the power button for about a second. A message appears onscreen asking you to confirm that you really want to shut down. To give your Fire a nap (and avoid having to power up again), press the power button ever so briefly; the screen goes dark. When you want to wake the Fire, press the button again and swipe the yellow unlock arrow.

Charging the Fire is simple. Plug the power cord into a standard electric wall socket and connect the USB dongle to the opening on the Fire that matches it. A full charge takes about four hours this way; you can also refill by plugging into a computer, but this method works more slowly. To check how much juice remains, in the Status bar (page 22), tap Quick Settings→More and then scroll down to and tap Device, where you see a quick report listing the figure in percentage terms. Two other ways to tell: The power button glows red when charging (and green when finished), and the Status bar's battery icon turns fully green when charging is done. During a charge, it pulses to indicate the fill-up's in progress.

TIP   Don't like your Fire's assigned name (*Gertrude's 7th Kindle*)? It's what appears on the upper-left corner of the screen, as well as on Amazon's various ebook, music, and media stores when you're asked which device you want to send your purchase to. Name-changing is easy. On Amazon.com, use the home page's left-hand Shop All Departments menu to navigate to Kindle→Manage Your Kindle. On the left side of the page that appears, click Manage Your Devices and then click the Edit link next to your Fire's currently assigned name. Enter the new name you want in the pop-up window and then click Update. Patience is the final requirement: It may take a few hours for your new handle to appear on the Fire.

The Home Screen

The home screen is the entry point to all the fun stuff on your Fire. If the Fire were a regular computer, here's where you'd find its desktop, control panel, application launcher, and search tool...all crammed onto one screen. There's a certain elegance to the layout here: As crowded as your Fire may some day become with ebooks, apps, tunes, and TV shows, you can always count on this screen's navigational simplicity. Head to toe, here's what your newest gadget looks like:

Status Bar

Quick Settings

Content Libraries

Favorites

Carousel

- **The Status bar.** Most of what's here is strictly read-only: your Fire's name, the time, the strength of your WiFi connection (represented by the industry standard stack-of-curved-lines icon), and a battery charge indicator (filled with white when you're fully charged; green when you're charging and plugged in). You may sometimes also see, on the left side, a number inside a circle: This Notifications circle is how apps, and the Fire itself, signal they've got a message for you—a new tweet or email awaits, for example. It's tappable, as is the gear-shaped Quick Settings icon on the right side.

That gear is the secret door to all sorts of custom controls. Tap it, and down drops a panel of frequently needed virtual settings: *Locked/Unlocked* (to prevent, or allow, the screen's contents from rotating as you turn the device horizontally or vertically); *Volume* (plus music controls, if you've got a tune playing); *Brightness* (of the screen's display); *Wi-Fi* (quick access to nearby networks); *Sync* (coordinates where you are in the ebook you're reading, or show you're watching, so you can pick up in the same spot on another device); and the overstuffed *More* option. This last one is covered choice-by-choice in Appendix A; you'll also meet its options on an as-needed basis throughout the main chapters of this book. Basically, it's the Fire's equivalent of Windows' Control Panel or the Mac's System Preferences.

- **The search oval.** On Day One this lookup tool may not get much of a work-out—what have you got to hunt for? But as you fill up Fire, it's a handy way to quickly find what you need. Depending on which tab you touch after tapping the oval—Library or Web—you're poking through your own collection (of songs, books, TV shows, and so on) or the Internet at large.

- **Content Libraries.** Each of the seven links in this row puts you one tap away from the Fire's starring lineup: Newsstand, Books, Music, Video, Docs, Apps, and Web. Each of these precincts gets its own chapter in the pages ahead. Enter any of them to either play with your collection or shop in the dedicated stores.

- **The Carousel.** A horizontally swipeable list of shortcut icons to items you've recently looked at: a book, an app, a TV show, or anything else on the Fire. A single tap launches whatever the icon represents. What's here is whatever's in the Fire's recent memory. In other words, the system decides what's on this shelf, not you. First time Fire starters will see an Amazon-penned user's guide (helpful, but containing none of the gems you get in a, um, *real* guidebook), a welcome note from Amazon CEO Jeff Bezos, and a list of any ebooks you've bought from his ebook shop, the Kindle Store.

  Move through this carousel by holding down and tracing your finger right to left. A light touch is all it takes; you can also flick, just as you'd do when spinning a Lazy Susan: The touchscreen plays along and delivers more or less momentum, depending on how fast you flick. Notice the little white downward-pointing arrow on the lower-right corner of any ebook cover. That means the item is sitting up on Amazon's servers; to download it, simply tap anywhere on the cover. After it downloads, tap it again, and the book appears onscreen. To get rid of anything on the Carousel, hold your finger on its icon and, from the pop-up menu, pick Remove from Carousel.

TIP You can get back to the home screen from pretty much anywhere by tapping the middle of any app, ebook, movie, and so on; the Options bar pops up at the bottom of the Fire, and on its far left side is the Home icon. Tap it and you're back on the main page. The universal back button—a leftward-pointing arrow—is also a handy navigational tool to know about. Tap it to return to whichever screen you just came from. Finally, pretty much every app has a Menu button; tap it to expose a row or two of further options, tailored to each app.

★★★★☆ (2 reviews)

4. Understanding Illuminated Manuscripts: A

Wish List	Cart
Your Account	About	Help

Home Back Menu

- **Favorites.** Here's your turn to play home page designer. Put one-tap icons to all your favorite apps, ebooks, web pages—even playlists (page 133). If you can view it on the Kindle, you can stick it on this shelf. Create as many of these one-tap-and-you're-there bookmarks as you like. (More shelves get added as you need 'em.) The quickest way: Start looking or listening to anything and, when its icon appears in the Carousel, tap and hold its icon till the Add to Favorites option appears. Feel like redecorating? Tap, hold, and drag any icon to reposition it. Or clean out your shelves by tapping, holding, and choosing "Remove from Favorites."

Now's a good time to mention two ways to protect your Fire from prying eyes and over-enthusiastic fingers. To require a password before letting anyone onto the home screen, head to Quick Settings→More→Security and set Lock Screen Password to On. Enter, confirm again the password you want, and then tap Finish. Now anyone who turns on or wakes up your Fire will need to enter the secret code. Four choices up from Security sits Restrictions. This gate-keeping feature is handy for parents who want to let their kids use the Fire to read books or play with apps, but prevent them from getting online or buying apps. It works by slapping a passcode lock on the WiFi network. To do that, turn the sole entry in Restrictions—Enable Restrictions—On and then create a password using the process just described for Security. Next time you hand over your Fire to Junior, turn off WiFi (Quick Settings→WiFi→Off) and he'll stay offline.

Tapping, Touching, Typing

You know how to tap. But don't be embarrassed if all the other, not-so-obvious touchscreen gestures seem foreign. That includes the flick, the swipe, the pinch, the twist, and—they don't call it *multi*-touch for nothing—those two-fingered maneuvers. Here, then, is a brief primer:

- **Tapping.** The touchscreen equivalent of mouse clicking. For icons and hyperlinks, a single tap is all you need. On web pages, photos, and some apps, double-tapping enlarges the spot where your finger hit. Double-tap again to return to the regular, full-page view. (Keep in mind that double-tapping doesn't *always* make things bigger; when using the Kindle app to read ebooks, for example, that gesture has no effect; page 43 shows how to use the Options bar to bump up the font size.)

- **Swiping.** Here's where you hold and trace your finger in either direction, left or right. Great for reviewing long rows of book covers, albums, and movies. If you swipe-and-release quickly, the items whiz along, till the software-simulated friction slows them down. Same as Vanna White spinning the big Wheel of Fortune.

- **Flicking.** Basically, vertical swiping. Any time you see a long, scrolling list (contacts, song titles) you can skim by moving the top of your finger quickly up- or downward. As in all touch gestures, use the fleshy tip of your finger here, not the nail (which will work, but is much harder to position).

- **The two-finger spread.** There isn't any real-world equivalent to this gesture, but somehow the way it works makes sense: Take two fingers (typically the thumb and pointer), put them down on the screen next to each other, and spread them apart. This move almost always enlarges what's onscreen. Very popular among photo and drawing apps.

- **The pinch.** Sometimes called the *reverse spread*, since it's the previous gesture rewound. On any bit of content that's been enlarged, place two fingers a chicken wing or so apart from each other and then pull them together. Now you get to see more stuff onscreen, albeit in a shrunken state.

The Keyboard

Voice recognition may be the future of gadget control, but the microphone-free Fire will ignore you no matter how loud you shout. Typing, then, is how you conduct searches, compose emails, and craft status updates. The downside of touchscreen typing on a relatively small device is the cramped keyboard; even a puny netbook gives you bigger tiles to press. The good news: Smart software powers the Fire's virtual keyboard. With time-saving assists like auto-completion suggestions, keyboard labels that adjust on-the-fly to match options you're most likely to need, and some simple auto-correct fixes, you'll probably find this input method easy to master.

NOTE What follows is an all-purpose guide to keyboarding. Many apps add custom frills, like a dedicated *.com* button in the web browser's keyboard.

The home screen's search bar is a good place to take the keyboard for a spin. Tap anywhere inside its oval, and up pops a five-row keyboard on the bottom of the screen. It works just as you might expect. Tap any key to type. As you do so, the keyboard sprouts a reminder, above and to the left of wherever you've just tapped, of the key you pressed. It's meant to spare you the trouble of having to look up and double check the top of the screen after each tap. Make a mistake?

The Delete key on the far right edge erases one character each time you hit it. Tap the Shift key once to summon an upper-case layout that sticks around for the next letter only. Tap the Shift key twice and the capital lineup sticks around till you dismiss it by tapping the Shift key again.

To get those tiny numbers perched in the upper-right corner of the top letter row, just tap and hold any host letter. Tap and hold *q*, for example, and you see an orange *1* sprout up; remove your finger to insert the number. (Change your mind? Drag your finger away till the orange key turns gray; now it won't enter anything in the text box.)

Above the letters, a row of common punctuation marks—exclamation point, question mark, and so on—are arranged for quick access. Other useful punctuation marks are hidden under the period (.) key. Touch and hold it to see a dozen or so items: semicolon, plus sign, ampersand, and so on.

TIP Turns out a bunch of letters sport secret, tucked away variations. Touch and hold the *a* for the most common accented varieties: à á â ã ä å ā æ. Other multipurpose keys include: e, y, u, i, o, s, c, and n.

You can find other, less popular variations (asterisk, pound sign) by tapping the lower-left corner's *123!?* key. Burrow even further down to more options (the British pound, the Euro, squiggly brackets) by tapping the *123!?* key and then, on the screen that appears, tap the *•+=* key. Return from any of these odd-key expeditions by tapping the lower-left corner's *ABC* key.

To edit a word you've already typed—for example, fixing the typo *ckngress*—tap (but don't hold) the spot you want to fix. You don't have to hit the exact letter, because you get an orange pointer that you can reposition by dragging, if it's not exactly where you want it. When it's positioned correctly—in front of the *k*— tap the keyboard's Delete key and then insert an *o* to fix the mistake.

> **NOTE** Want to customize a handful of keyboard settings, like the sounds it makes when tapped and whether or not new sentences automatically start with a capital letter? Page 245 has the scoop.

Installing Apps

Apps are a big reason people buy tablets and smartphones. Short for *applications*, these downloadable programs turn your Fire into a 21st-century Swiss Army knife. Play games, edit photos, brush up on your Shakespeare—the list of what these single-purpose programs can do is almost endless. Amazon's store (officially called the Amazon Appstore for Android) is where you shop for, or download for free, these goodies.

The simplest way to get an app is by heading to the Apps Library and tapping the Store link. Use the search oval to look for a specific title, or browse either of the Top Paid and Free lists. There's also a horizontally swipeable list of sub-categories: New, Games, Entertainment, and so on.

Once you've spotted an app you want, click its orange download button (either the one that says Free or lists a price). The button turns green (saying either Get or Buy App); tap it again to start the download. After the download is complete, the button morphs one last time and now says Open. Tap it to launch the app. Throughout this book you'll meet apps that beef up what your Fire can do. And the final three chapters focus exclusively on helping you pick the best apps in popular, crowded categories like games and task trackers.

You can also go app picking from a computer's web browser. One advantage to this route is that you get some fine-tuned browsing options that aren't available on the Fire's built-in app store. For example, in the "Available on Kindle

Fire" section of the web-based store (*http://amzn.to/kfmm131*) you can turn on a checkbox (left-hand column) showing just the free apps. When you've found an app you want, click its "Buy now" or "Get now" button (the second is for freebies). In a minute or so, a new message appears in your Fire's Notifications circle (page 22), letting you know your new app's ready for download. Tap the link that says "New Apps Available" and, from the list that appears, hit the Install button next to whatever you just downloaded.

If you're getting impatient and haven't got word of the app's arrival, you can nudge the Fire to check for available downloads. Tap the Apps Library link, followed by the upper-right Store button. Then go to Options bar→Menu→My Apps and tap the upper-right Refresh button.

TIP Got your eyes on an Android app that's *not* listed in Amazon's Appstore? If you see an app listed in the Android Market or other app retailer, you can grab and install *some* titles (but not all; Google's own official apps are a notable exception). Be ready, though, for a little software spelunking. The how-to blog *Tested* has a nice guide: *http://bit.ly/kfmm106*.

Cloud vs. Device

Many early Fire reviews agreed: 8 gigabytes of storage was somewhere between skimpy and scandalous. With a device that's *supposed* to be a portable media center, how on earth can you cram everything into that meager space?

You can't. But you don't have to.

Enter *the Cloud*, this decade's frontrunner for most overused bit of jargon. As you've probably figured out, the term refers to stuff stored up on the Internet. Geeks appreciate how the Cloud matches the Internet illustrations in their diagrams. Marketing types get excited because terms like *online* and *web-based* were getting boring.

To be fair, though, Cloud-based offerings do contain some special qualities. For starters, any digital file that's stored in the Cloud is automatically available on *any* of the devices you own or happen to be using (a PC at the library, for example). That means any Kindle book you've ever bought is ready for downloading and reading on any Kindle gadget or app. Same goes, more or less, for Amazon's TV shows and movies. (The "less" being that you can't watch a movie on your first-generation Kindle.) In a world where most people shuttle between multiple computers, tablets, and smartphones, having widespread, easy access to all this media is a *huge* convenience.

Amazon takes the concept a bit further with its Whispersync service. With Whispersync, not only is that John Grisham thriller you're reading available on any Kindle reader, but your bookmarks, notes, and even your reading location are coordinated everywhere. Start reading on the commute home using a BlackBerry, and then pick up where you left off on your Fire when you crawl into bed. Backup worries also get washed away. No longer do you have to go through the tedium of all that copying. As long as you believe that Amazon's here to stay—probably a safe bet—their pledge is that you can always re-download anything you bought from them.

For Fire owners, the Cloud plays an even bigger role. It gives you access to loads more media than can actually fit on your machine. With a mere 6 gigabytes of available storage space, it won't come close to holding the 20 GB-plus music collections that many folks have accumulated. And forget about those digital movie libraries. At around 2 GB for each title, you wouldn't get halfway through the *Star Wars* saga.

Amazon's solution? Setting you up with a healthy sized Cloud-based shelf. You can enjoy anything stored there, as long as you have a WiFi connection. Tap any of the main Libraries (music, books, and so on), and you'll notice two tabs at the top of each library's screen: Device and Cloud. Here lie the routes to whatever you want to play or view. Files behind door number one reside directly on the Fire itself. Door number two—the Cloud—is what lives on Amazon's virtual drives. Whenever you and your Fire are inside a reasonably speedy WiFi zone, everything you see there is showtime ready.

Now, of course, there are some catches:

- **Moving your files online.** For ebooks, apps, TV shows, and movies, this one's a non-issue. Buy any of those items from Amazon, and the digital files await online forevermore and automatically. Music's another story. If you've built your collections from iTunes purchases or burning lots of CDs, you'll need to spend time hauling those bits from local hard drive to the one in the Cloud. Guidance on how to make that happen begins on page 121. (If you've bought your tunes from Amazon, you're covered. All its MP3 files get stored there once you flip on a single checkbox; details on page 124.)

- **No or poor WiFi connection.** Remotely stored media is only convenient if you can get to it. If you're a subway-riding city slicker, ranch hand far out on the range, or an airplane-trapped traveler, you may not have a WiFi signal in reach.

- **Everything Amazon.** It's getting increasingly difficult these days to live a life that doesn't depend on one of the following firms: Amazon, Apple, Facebook, or Google. By storing all or most of your digital stuff on Amazon's servers, you're making it tough to pack up and take your media business somewhere else. And it's not simply a logistical challenge you'd face. In plenty of cases—ebooks, TV shows, and movies—you *can't* take those files with you. They've got software locks attached (DRM, short for *digital rights management*) that make the files playable only on Amazon-controlled software and gadgets.

- **Cost.** Amazon's starter cloud package is free and reasonably sized (5 giga-bytes, no charge for those tunes purchased on their music store). But if you stick with Amazon, you'll probably find yourself ponying up for additional space. All your options are described starting on page 124, but given the annual fees for this extra space, it's a price worth understanding.

Fact is, though, however many downsides you can think of, with only 8 gigs on the Fire, sooner or later you'll have to pick what deserves on-device stor-age and what's okay to keep in Cloudville. Of course there's no right or wrong approach. A few items are no-brainers for bringing onto the Fire: the ebook you're currently reading, plus the handful of Best Books Ever; reference works (cookbooks, for example) that would be great to have while at that cabin in the woods; any movies you want to watch on a long flight; the couple hundred greatest hits in your music and photo library; and your essential document col-lection. It helps that the Fire makes it pretty easy to flush out what you don't need and download what you do.

TIP To keep tabs on how much room you've got left, check out Quick Settings→Device→Internal Storage.

So there you have it: a short version of Cloud 101. Ready to go have some fun with your Fire? Reading books is a great place to start, which is what the next chapter covers in detail.

CHAPTER 2

Reading Books

AMAZON CEO JEFF BEZOS has always had one big design goal for the Kindle: to make it "disappear in your hands so you can enjoy your reading." Even though the Fire's the heaviest, most feature-packed model in the family, it meets its dad's main objective. Whether you're a Kindle veteran, an occasional smartphone reader, or even a hardcover lover, you'll find it easy to read on the Fire.

Two things in particular make the Fire a good alternative to print. First: choice. There may be bigger online catalogs, but no one beats Amazon when it comes to titles people actually want to read. Google's eBookstore, for example, boasts three million titles—and those are just the free ones! But if you ever wade deep into those virtual stacks, you'll find lots of shoddily scanned snooze inducers. Meanwhile, Amazon has deals in place with more or less every publisher around. And thanks to its own fast-growing editorial operation, the lineup of Amazon-only authors—early names include Tim Ferris and Seth Godin—is impressive.

The Fire's second big attraction is Amazon's focus on the reading experience. When historians write up the tectonic shift from print to digital, the company may well get blamed for bound books' diminished profile. But it also deserves kudos for sweating the little things that make ebook-reading an immersive experience. Things like distraction-free page design, avoiding intrusive "social" frills, and reading software that really does get out of the way and let you read. Ready to read some books? This chapter shows you how.

NOTE Comic book fans, a few apps await to help indulge your habit; the Tip on page 58 has the scoop on one leading option: the Comics app. And dozens of Fire-friendly graphic novels—specially formatted to accommodate the slightly smaller screen—are available, too. They get their own category in the Kindle Bookstore (Comics & Graphic Novels); see page 55 for more on how to navigate its aisles.

Grab a Book

If you've ever bought an ebook from Amazon, your path to its pages is short. As long as you used the same Amazon account (page 19) to both buy that title and register the Fire, the book's waiting for you either on the home screen's Carousel (page 23), or inside the Books Library. (There, you may need to tap the Cloud tab and then tap the book's cover again to download, or it may be already sitting in the Device section, ready to read.)

If you don't yet own a Kindle book (which is what Amazon sometimes calls its ebooks), see page 55 for how to download one so you can follow along for the next few pages. The short version: On the Fire, go to Books→Store, scroll down to the bottom of the screen, and tap one of the free books listed there.

Page Turning and Navigation

What you see onscreen when opening a book depends on whether you're cracking its spine for the first time or have dipped into it before. The first time, you see the publisher's chosen kickoff page—often the page right after the table of contents. After that initial launch, the book opens to where you left off.

Either way, turning pages works the same. Tap anywhere on the right side of the page (an inch or so from the edge is the hot zone) to move ahead one page. Swiping from right to left *anywhere* does the same. You can hold your finger and drag while doing this, or, if you're in a hurry, simply flick your finger leftward. To move backwards, one page at a time, reverse any of these gestures. Tap anywhere on the left side of the page (the same one-inch margin) or swipe/flick from left to right.

THE INTERROGATIVE MOOD

on the head of a pin? Do you have long-term friends whom you assume are friends for life who suddenly abandon you, as it were, or at any rate declare one way or another that it won't be "friends for life" after all? Do you struggle against this attrition or do you accept it as part of the wholesale attrition of aging? Do you have any of your school report cards or childhood athletic trophies? Is the bone around the eye socket called the occipital bone or occipital socket or something like that? Would you pick up a lamprey eel or a hellbender? If you could grow your own coffee, would you? Have you ever managed to pet a chicken? Does the wholesale attrition of aging become in effect your not caring about much, or conceivably anything, the way you once might have, and do you see yourself finally caring about nothing at all or do you see yourself taking a stand for a few things, as though you might be heading for your own private senile Alamo? Do you remember the custom automotive gas pedal that resembled a large bare chrome human foot? Were you ever whipped with a belt or a hairbrush? At what age would you say your character was set—that is, when do you think you were you? Out of all the times in your life you have wept, can you select a time that you most wish you had not wept? Are you as fond as I of cobalt glass?

May I ask you to picture a garter snake eating a Christmas ornament and dying from it as a preliminary to subsequent questions I may or may

TIP You can tap and swipe to move between a graphic novel's pages, too. But let's face it: Most of the dialog in those big-print-page originals is tough to read on the Fire's smaller screen. That's where Kindle Panel View comes in—Amazon's panel-magnifying and quick navigation tool. Double-tap any panel to summon it. Then, simply tap anywhere on the screen's right edge. The Fire automatically serves up the next panel. Keep tapping, and you'll get a specially magnified tour of the whole book. Panel View is even smart enough to pop up the top-left panel when you start a new page. To return to regular reading mode, double-tap anywhere on the screen.

Tap anywhere in the middle of the page to summon the Options bar at bottom (more on that in a moment) and the Location slider. If you're new to Kindle-land, here's the location lowdown. Ebooks and page numbers don't get along very well. That's because you, dear reader, are free to adjust font size. So what began as, say, page 27 pre-bigification, is now some *other* page number. And, whatever the text size, what you see onscreen on that hypothetical page 27 has absolutely no connection to the same page number in a print book.

Amazon's solution: *Location numbering*. In this system, each chunk of text (128 bytes, for those scoring at home) gets assigned a number. The first one you see listed in the Location slider—for example, *1456 of 4856*—is the chunk at the top of the page; the second one's the last bit of the book. Your progress also gets displayed in percentage terms. A print book that has, say, 627 pages, in its Kindle edition would span from Location 1 to 12477. Now that you know *why* it's there, operating the slider's the easy part: Just drag the dot in either direction to move around the book.

NOTE   You say you *have* spotted Kindle books with page numbers? You're not going crazy: Some publishers, with Amazon's cooperation, embed print page number equivalents that coordinate digital and physical editions. However, not all publishers do the extra work that page numbering requires. And Amazon includes this feature only on certain Kindle devices and apps, a list which, for now, doesn't include the Fire.

You can find other ways to move around a book by tapping the Menu icon (the three horizontal lines) that appears when you touch the middle of the screen. From there you can go to:

- **Cover.** Most publishers place a digital replica of the front of the print jacket here. Sometimes that looks fine, other times it looks like...a print production crammed onto a too-small screen. Fact is, ebook covers are still a developing art form.

- **Table of Contents.** Most publishers include one; some don't. What you get, if it's there, is a hyperlinked version of what appears in a print book. Tap to navigate to any chapter or sub-section. If the TOC (as it's sometimes abbreviated) is too long to fit on one screen, then page ahead just as you would with any other page in the ebook.

- **Beginning.** A publisher-designated starting line. Usually this is the first page of honest-to-goodness text, but thorough readers, beware. Epitaphs and dedications often appear before this point, so if you want the full beginning-to-end experience, start at the cover.

- **Location.** Tap to enter any number to go to that location (line). This option often leaves print fans scratching their heads. Why the heck would you ever want to go to, say, Location 1189? Well, if you have Kindle book-reading pals, it's one way to communicate specific reading spots. And if you ever find yourself embarking on a virtual page flipping expedition (returning to the opening pages of a novel to reread a passage) you can make a mental note of your location and use this tool to quickly "flip back" there. Another alternative: Set a bookmark, as explained on page 45.

- **Sync to Furthest Page.** If you read the same book on multiple devices (a PC at work, a BlackBerry during your commute, and so on), Amazon has answered your device-coordination prayers. It's called Whispersync—a way to manually move all your devices to the same page. Just tap this link. (The full explanation lies ahead on page 48.)

- **My Notes & Marks.** Any highlight or note you make gets added to this list (situated below the previous options when your Kindle is upright and to your right if you're holding the device's short edges). Tap any entry to navigate to its position within the book. Bookmarks get listed here, too. Page 44 shows how to add all these items.

TIP Some books have graphics or other illustrations. To get a fullscreen view, double-tap the image, which now appears all by itself on the screen. You can pinch and spread (page 25) to zoom in and out. Tap the upper-right X to return to regular reading.

The Back Button

Back button

This button offers a special magic—an instant return path after you've tapped an in-book link (a footnote, say). Read the author's aside or citation—usually sequestered somewhere toward the back of the book—and then tap the Back button. If you don't see it, you can summon it by tapping anywhere in the middle of the screen. The Back button whisks you to the spot you departed from. What can sometimes get confusing is distinguishing its role from the go-back methods explained on page 36. Those take you back one screen at a time. The Back button returns you from any link you've visited. In fact, it's the *same* Back button that sits on call at the bottom of almost every Fire app. So even if an ebook link shoots you off to the Web, just tap the browser's Back button, and you return to the reading location you departed from.

Search and...Research

An inch or so to the right of the Back button, the search monocle sits ready to train its powers on any book you're reading. Tap it, enter any word or phrase, and then hit Go. In the results list that appears, the Fire highlights the found term in yellow (as it does on the actual page, if you tap a search result).

Want to widen the scope of your search area *outside* the book? Tap-and-hold any word. The window that pops up gives a dictionary's quick take—see the full definition by hitting the link of that name. Behind the More button are links that search either Wikipedia or Google. Both tools make it simple to do a quick bit of research and then get back to reading. Pages from both sites appear on a stripped-down web browser built right into the Kindle reading app. It's a distraction-free lens onto the Web—no bookmarks, no web address bar—a subtle reminder that reading, and not web surfing, is the main event.

cluttered with scripts in Russian, Arabic, Chinese and English. Xinjiang is an outpost, lying beyond the deserts and mountains of Gansu Province. In

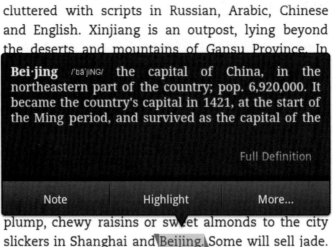

Bei·jing /ˈbāˈjiNG/ the capital of China, in the northeastern part of the country; pop. 6,920,000. It became the country's capital in 1421, at the start of the Ming period, and survived as the capital of the

Full Definition

Note   Highlight   More...

plump, chewy raisins or sweet almonds to the city slickers in Shanghai and Beijing. Some will sell jade. I imagine them bartering for their jade by dark of

If the info you need is on the web page you've been taken to, returning to your reading spot is simple: Tap the Back button. (You can also tap the Menu icon to expose a Back to Reading icon.) If you click a link pointing to another site, on either the Wikipedia or the Google results page, you'll get shifted over to the Fire's full-fledged web browser (page 173). Should your expedition onto the Web take you across several links, click the Back button for each link you've followed, and you'll eventually return to where you were in your ebook.

NOTE If you're serious about searching, you may notice a bug that, alas, as of this writing, has no simple fix. If the word you're interested in is followed by a quotation mark or footnote (*...hippocampus."*), there's no way to select only the word itself. No matter how much you try adjusting those selection arrows, you get the whole glob. That puts the kibosh on getting a dictionary definition. It also monkeys with your Google and Wikipedia searches (which, of course, you can perform manually, but who wants to take time doing *that?*).

Playing Page Designer

Ebooks are a boon to readers with fading eyesight. All it takes is a tap or two to bump up the text's size. Presto, you've got a large-type edition. The Fire's loaded with ways to customize what you see onscreen. Tap the Option bar's *Aa* icon to get a look at your two-tabbed design palette. Typeface, on the right, is straightforward: Seven choices appear, ranging from Arial to Trebuchet. Font Style is where you can really tailor your text:

- **Font size.** From microscopic to jumbotronic, these eight settings should satisfy most eyes.

- **Line spacing.** Bunch the lines tightly together or give 'em room to breathe.

- **Margins.** Here's where you control how much space surrounds the text. (By the way, while each setting's icon suggests that adjustments will happen on all four margins, the only ones that *actually* shift are left and right.)

- **Color mode.** Three flavors: black text on a white background; white text on black; or dark brown on light.

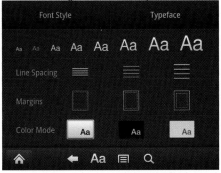

Screen brightness is another key factor in readability. Studies show that onscreen brightness is best when it matches the room's surrounding light. In other words: A really bright screen in an otherwise dark room is murder on your eyes. To turn the backlight up or down, tap the screentop Quick Settings icon and, from the drop-down menu, adjust the Brightness slider.

> **TIP** Reading a heavily illustrated kids book? (One clue: Its only layout option is horizontal. Even if you rotate the Fire vertically, the content doesn't budge.) Enlarge any text box by tapping it; repeat to shrink it back down to its original size. You may not always need this temporary magnifier, but if the type's extra small, you can use it to help readers-in-training.

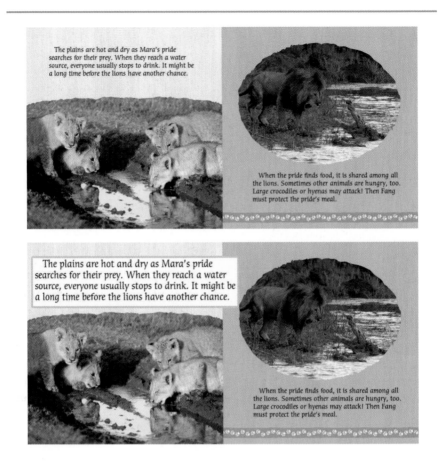

The plains are hot and dry as Mara's pride searches for their prey. When they reach a water source, everyone usually stops to drink. It might be a long time before the lions have another chance.

When the pride finds food, it is shared among all the lions. Sometimes other animals are hungry, too. Large crocodiles or hyenas may attack! Then Fang must protect the pride's meal.

The plains are hot and dry as Mara's pride searches for their prey. When they reach a water source, everyone usually stops to drink. It might be a long time before the lions have another chance.

When the pride finds food, it is shared among all the lions. Sometimes other animals are hungry, too. Large crocodiles or hyenas may attack! Then Fang must protect the pride's meal.

Notes and Highlighting

Taking notes and highlighting passages are indispensable tools to some readers (you know who you are). Both are great for flagging an author's most astute points—or spotlighting boneheaded claims. To do either on the Fire:

❶ **Select the passage you want to highlight or attach a note to.** Start by pressing and holding your finger on the first word you want to select. A magnifying rectangle previews what's beneath your finger (which would otherwise be hard to see). Without pulling your finger off the screen, drag over or down to the last word; a pair of selection triangles surrounds the text. Don't worry if you don't grab exactly what you want; reposition either triangle to lengthen or shorten the selection.

another stone, were as rudimentary as the scribbles of toddlers. Eventually the drawings became more realistic, outlining the actual proportions of a space,

| Note | Highlight | More... |

realism became scientific in both its precision and its abstraction. The mapmaker began to use sophisticated tools like the direction-finding compass and the angle-measuring theodolite and to rely on mathematical reckonings and formulas. Eventually, in a further intellectual leap, maps came to be used not only to represent vast regions of the

❷ **From the pop-up menu that appears, decide whether you want to write a note or add a highlight.** Notetakers: After jotting down your thoughts, tap the Save button on the right edge of the text entry box. To get rid of (or edit) a note, tap quickly the blue there's-a-note-here icon. From the pop-up box that appears, choose whether to change or delete what you've written. This pop-up box is also one way to view a note; page 39 describes a common gathering spot for all your notes and the box on page 46 profiles a web-based repository. To delete highlights, hold anywhere on the yellow region; a contextual bar sprouts up and the middle option is Delete Highlight.

NOTE Some Kindle veterans may wonder what happened to the Twitter and Facebook sharing option that Amazon unveiled in mid-2011. It hasn't yet made its way to the Fire, but it's hard to imagine this remaining so for very long.

Bookmarks

Bookmarks are a kind of sidekick to notes and highlights, and they're a snap to add. Tap the center of any page and, in the upper-right corner, tap the translucent gray ribbon (repeat to remove it). To return to any bookmarked location, tap the Menu button (page 23) and look for any blue-ribbon icon; tap it and you're back to where you inserted it.

Highlights and Notes To Go

One of the most frustrating aspects of the major ebook systems—Kindle included—are their stingy sharing policies. They don't make it easy to borrow and lend ebooks (for some exceptions, see page 59). But why must publishers keep our own notes chained to these books, when all you want is to use that commentary to write a paper, compose a blog post, or dump into a reading journal? Turns out you can copy notes made on your Kindle but you have to make a separate trip to the Web. Visit the Amazon Kindle site (*http:// kindle.amazon.com*) and, lo and behold, every single note you've made or passage you've highlighted shows up here. To grab anything, simply select and copy as you would any web page text. It's not the most elegant solution in the world, but it works. A few other fun tricks you might want to try out on this site:

- **Follow other people.** Amazon has supplied a neat tool for peeking over the shoulders of friends and famous people alike—you get to see what books they've read, which ones they want to read, and even the annotations they've made. All this is strictly opt-in, of course: People have to choose to participate, which they (or you) can do by visiting the Your Books section of the Kindle site listed in the previous paragraph. From there, turn on two checkboxes next to the books whose notes you wish to make peekable: "Make

Reading Status & Rating Public" and "Public Notes: Make Yours Public." To find someone to follow, on that site's home page, either enter her name in the site's Search box or click either the Twitter or Facebook links in the "Find People You Know" section.

- **Daily review.** Want a periodic refresher of books you've already read? This flashcard-style offering serves up a small portion of any Kindle book you've marked up. What you see on this web page are passages you've highlighted, plus any notes you've made. Dip back into the full book by installing the PC- or Mac-based Kindle software. Clicking the Amazon Kindle site's excerpt takes you directly to the spot in the book where the passage is from.

- **Track all your books.** The Your Books link at the top of the Amazon Kindle site is command central for all books that Amazon knows you're interested in—Kindle and print. It's their nascent version of a book-tracking site (kinda like Goodreads or the Amazon-owned Shelfari). Add titles to this list by using the upper-right Search box to find them. You can also indicate reading status (Read, Reading, Hope to Read, Stopped Reading), rate the book, and decide how much of all this gets shared publicly.

Daily Review

Hurry Down Sunshine
by Michael Greenberg

" acute cases of psychosis. Haloperidol is a direct descendant of chlorpromazine, the ur-drug of the psychopharmacological age. Its psychiatric value is its ability to induce indifference. ("The chemical lobotomy," psychiatrists called it when it was introduced in 1952, referring to the procedure that it rendered obsolete: the severing of nerve fibers in the brain's frontal lobes with a household ice "

Note: Add a note

Go to your Daily Review

Your Books

Filter: ⦿ **All** (68) ○ Read (15) ○ Reading (6) ○ Hope to read (47) ○ Stopped reading (0)

< Previous | Page: **1** 2 3 | Next >   Display: Kindle Only ⬍

BOOK # / AUTHOR	READING STATUS	YOUR RATING	MAKE READING STATUS & RATING PUBLIC	PUBLIC NOTES: MAKE YOURS PUBLIC	REMOVE FROM LIST
5 Very Good Reasons to Punch a Dolphin in the Mouth (And Other Useful Guides) Matthew Inman	Read	★★★★☆✕	☐	☐	⊗
African Cats: A Lion's Pride Disney Book Group	Hope to Read	☆☆☆☆☆	☐	☐	⊗
Art & Fear: Observations on the Perils (and Rewards) of Artmaking David Bayles, Ted Orland	Read	★★★★☆✕	☑	☑	⊗

Your Highlights (Most recently updated first)

Art & Fear: Observations on the Perils (and Rewards) of Artmaking by David Bayles, Ted Orland
You have **28** highlighted passages
You have **3** notes
Last annotated on November 26, 2011

Making the work you want to make means finding nourishment within the work itself. Read more at location 72 ⬈ · Delete this highlight
Add a note

In large measure becoming an artist consists of learning to accept yourself, which makes your work personal, and in following your own voice, which makes your work distinctive. Read more at location 86 ⬈ · Delete this highlight
Add a note

talent is rarely distinguishable, over the long run, from perseverance and lots of hard work. Read more at location 87 ⬈ · Delete this highlight
Add a note

our flaws and weaknesses, while often obstacles to our getting work done, are a source of strength as well. Read more at location 98 ⬈ · Delete this highlight

NOTE   Two entries for the folks manning Fire's Missing Features Department: Book Extras and X-ray. Found in most other Kindle reading apps, the first is a handy Cliffs Notes–like collection of character summaries and key quotes—all pulled from the Shelfari book-tracking site. The extras aren't available for all books, but when they are there, they make for a handy memory refresher. The X-ray tool debuted in the fall of 2011 on the new touchscreen Kindle e-reading devices. Similar to Book Extras, this feature taps into Shelfari and serves up a neat looking visual of wherever a character, historical figure, place, or topic gets mentioned in a book. Who knows for sure, but both seemed destined to make it to the Fire at some point.

Reading on Multiple Devices

Even before there was Fire, there was sync. Or as Amazon calls it: Whispersync. (As opposed to, what, noisy sync?) Whatever its name, this service is *incredibly* handy. It works like this: Amazon's super-smart servers make sure that you're always in the same reading location, regardless of what hardware you're holding. Start reading at sunrise on your BlackBerry, switch over to your Fire during the bus ride, and then sneak in a few pages at work on your Dell laptop.

Behind the scenes, Amazon automatically coordinates your reading location, any notes you make, and any highlights and bookmarks you add. Each device in your fleet needs an Internet connection—not to mention a copy of the book. To make the latter happen, web browse over to Amazon's Manage Your Kindle page (Amazon.com→Your Account→Manage Your Kindle; *http://amzn.to/ kfmm113*) and, from the Actions menu next to any title you've purchased, pick from the "Deliver to my..." list. Next time you launch a Kindle app, the synched copy downloads. (The Fire, as well as the other Kindle devices that Amazon makes, often requires one further nudge: a trip to the Sync button, found on the Fire by visiting Status Bar→Settings.)

Amazon offers free Kindle reading apps for most computers and gadgets. The full list includes Android-powered phones, BlackBerry devices, iPhones, iPads, iPod Touches, Macs, Windows PCs and phones (version 7), and a web-browser tool called Kindle Cloud Reader (download it at: *http://amzn.to/kfmm103*). And, of course, there's every Kindle device that Amazon makes.

Gadget hoarder alert: Some publishers place a six-device limit on each ebook you buy from Amazon. That is, you can't simultaneously download any Kindle book to more than six different Kindle reading apps or devices. If you get a message warning you've reached that limit, it's time to nix one copy of the ebook from one of your e-reading devices.

All this is great when it works, which is most of the time. But things do, occasionally, get Whisper*stuck*. That can happen when:

- You have no Internet connection. If you take your Fire hiking and read 50 pages in *Jane Eyre*, how will the Kindle app on your Galaxy Nexus find out about your progress? It won't, at least not until the Fire gets back in WiFi range, at which point a couple things need to happen. First, the Fire's version of *Jane Eyre* needs to be open so that Whispersync can grab its latest info. And the Nexus needs to be open, too, to ingest those updates. If you're in a rush to switch from one device to the other, it helps to know about the Sync button. Tap it, and you tell Whispersync: "Hey, pal, sync now, please." (In most Kindle apps, look for a pair of arrows chasing each other's tails; on the Fire, head to the Quick Settings menu.)

- Your kid grabs your Fire and swipes ahead 100 pages or so on your copy of *How to Raise Your I.Q. by Eating Gifted Children*. Next time you pick up your iPhone it suddenly thinks you've actually read that far—and keeps asking if you want to "Go to the furthest place read?" every time you open any of your Kindle readers. How do you let Whispersync know where you *really* are? Unfortunately, there's no way to do so; you'll keep getting that prompt till you actually get to that 100-pages-ahead mark, at which point the Fire stops nudging you and you can stop scolding your kid.

Sometimes, you may want all this auto-syncing to stop. Maybe you don't like the idea of Amazon peering over your virtual shoulder as you read. And there's one other rare but real scenario: If you and someone else use the same Amazon account to download copies of a book (you to your Fire, your partner to a Droid, for example), then nix the syncing. That keeps you from jerking each other to the same reading spot.

To turn Whispersync off, use a web browser to log into the Amazon account you used to purchase the book you want to un-sync. Head to Manage Your Kindle→Manage Your Devices and in the Device Synchronization section, under the Actions header, click Turn Off.

Audiobooks

Mainly good news here, plus one small downer. Audible.com's entire catalog is Fire-ready. Makes sense, since Amazon owns Audible. All you need is the Audible app, which is conveniently pre-loaded on the Fire. To start listening, follow these steps:

❶ **Launch the Audible app.** You may find it on your home screen's Carousel (page 23). If not, go to the Apps library, tap the Device tab, and you'll see it listed there.

❷ **Sign in.** If you've got an existing account with the service, touch Sign In. You can set one up in the app or online at *www.audible.com*. Accounts are free to create and are required to download free titles or purchase books one at a time. Optional membership plans are available for heavy listeners who want volume discounts (see *http://bit.ly/kfmm104* for details). Newcomers can also tap "I'm new to Audible" to test-drive the app without handing over any of your personal info; on the screen that follows pick the country you're in and you'll be a tap away from some free excerpts.

> **TIP** Prefer using your Amazon user name and password for everything Audible? Log onto the latter's website, click "Account details," and then choose "Use your Amazon account on Audible." The steps that follow are simple and involve confirming your current Audible password, entering your Amazon account details, and confirming which credit card you want to use.

❸ **Download a title and start playing it.** If you opted for a test drive, you'll see a handful of samples waiting on the app's main My Library page. Each of those titles is stored on Audible's servers. Tap the download icon (a downward-pointing arrow) to the right of any book you want to hear. The arrow morphs into a Download button and then—you guessed it—tap again to commence downloading.

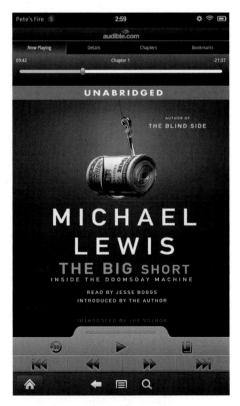

To play any download, tap its title in the My Library list. The file immediately starts playing, with the real stuff preceded by a grating corporate promo ("This Is Audible": gee, thanks). A familiar pause button sits at the bottom of the screen.

When you're ready to navigate forward or backward, there are plenty of ways to do so:

- **30 seconds back.** Just to the left of the pause button, this handy guy is great for popping back a half-minute if you get distracted. (Tip: You can change the amount of time on its face by heading back to the My Library screen, and then going to Options bar→Menu→Settings→Playback Settings→Back 30 Button. Enter any number of seconds, from 1 to 300.)

- **Forward fast, rewind.** Swipe up the pause button's gray bar. A full complement of familiar audio controls appear (from left to right): previous track, rewind, fast forward, next track. The first and last controls transport you from chapter to chapter. The middle two—rewind and fast forward—do what they say: Tap either once to spool at double speed (a 2x icon appears on whichever button you tap). Keep tapping to bump things up to 4x and 8x. Notice the time elapsed counter, just below the Now Playing tab. It tallies onward to reflect the track's new position. You won't immediately hear the audio going all squiggly as it accelerates forward or back; that happens after a few seconds.

- **The scrubber bar.** Laid out in yellow across the top of the screen, this bar lets you drag its gray location controller to adjust your position in the book. After tapping and holding the controller, keep your finger onscreen and drag downward to see different pacing options (hi-speed, half speed, quarter speed, fine scrubbing). The last one's great for second-by-second movement.

- **The Chapters tab.** Most publishers chunk up their works into individual chapters; here's where you navigate between these pieces.

- **Narrator Speed.** Attention Chipmunks fans. Head to the Menu icon (on the Options bar; page 23) and then pick Narrator Speed. Up pop six voice-speed control options: from half speed (0.5x) all the way to the high-pitched 3x.

- **Bookmarks.** Add as many of these as you like. Tap the bookmark icon to the right of the pause button. You can add a note too, if you like, in the pop-up window (or do nothing and it will disappear). Your collection gets stored in the Bookmarks tab.

- **Button-free.** This one looks a little weird at first, but it's a must-have for times when you can't fiddle with small buttons (like when you're driving). Tap the Menu icon and then pick Button-Free. A series of large-type navigational cues takes over your screen: Swipe Right to Go Forward 30s (seconds); Swipe Down to Go to Next Chapter; and so on. There's enough here for basic starting, stopping, and moving around. To return to Normalville, tap the Option bar's exposure triangle (tiny white thing, bottom of the screen) and then hit the universal Back button.

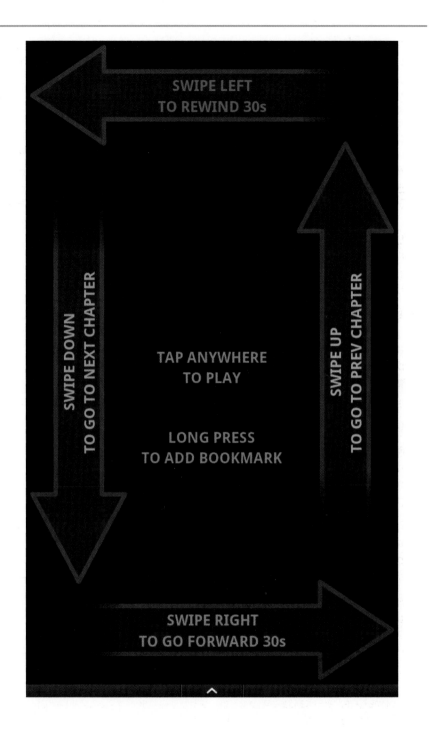

Shopping for Audiobooks

Wandering Audible.com's aisles, you won't lack for choice. This 15-year-old company stocks not just books but also magazines, comedy sketches, podcasts, and speeches. You can pick from pretty much all the bestsellers, plus oodles of novels, biographies, thrillers, Oprah's Book Club selections, even old-time radio shows. You can do your shopping from any web browser, although it's easier to find free stuff when using the Fire's Audible app (details on how to do that in a moment). If you do use a browser to buy, when you're back in the Audible app, click the upper-right Refresh button (curled arrow chasing its tail) on your My Library page. That pulls down any purchases you've made online.

To shop from within the app, start by tapping the shopping cart icon (which sits opposite the Refresh button). Browse using any of the big categories listed in the middle of the screen (Best Sellers, New Releases, Categories, and so on). Or enter a specific title in the search box. A Filter List button is buried a couple levels down in the Categories section. Head into any of the genres that appear in that grouping to further winnow down your results. Some of the filters you can apply include length, release date, and price; the latter's where you can show just the freebies.

Amazon's text-to-speech service, a weak alternative to Audible, didn't make it into Fire's feature lineup. This good-in-a-pinch tool debuted on some of the earlier Kindle hardware. It uses a computerized voice to recite an ebook's contents (assuming the publisher consented; some didn't, hoping audio fans would pony up for the audiobook edition).

There's no comparison between the two renditions. No one will ever mistake Donald Sutherland's narration of Hemingway's *The Old Man and the Sea* with a stilted silicon-powered voice. It would be nice, though, having the option, and for that Fire fans will have to wait.

Browsing and Buying

Kindle book shopping is simple, fun, and addictive. The free samples alone almost justify the cost of buying a low-end $79 Kindle or maybe even a Fire. You get the first five percent or so of *any* book, free to download and peruse. Back in olden times you had to trundle off to the library or your local bookshop. Now you can browse a wide selection of books wherever you have WiFi. You're only a hard-to-resist tap of the Buy button away—one that requires confrontation with neither cash nor credit card. No wonder Amazon gives you so many ways to do it:

- **From the Fire.** In the Books Library, tap the Store link. The page you see here is topped by a horizontally swipeable "Recommended for You" list. And then, below that, is a collection of ever-changing spotlights: New & Noteworthy, Top 100 Paid, Editor's Picks, and so on. On the right side of the main screen, don't miss the Browse Books link. Tap it to drill immediately down into the two dozen or so main book categories: Advice & How-to and Arts & Entertainment all the way through Sports and Travel. Touch any title to see a page dedicated to it. You see the same information as on Amazon.com: a "Try a Sample" button, a summary of the book, customer reviews, publication info, file size, and length (in print).

Those personal recommendations don't always match your actual interests. Sometimes a recent buying spree—for your eight year-old niece's birthday, say—can skew the results. To nudge things in the right direction, pay a visit to Amazon's Kindle book-specific Recommended for You web page. (Start out on the front page of the Kindle eBooks section and, halfway down the left edge, you'll see Your Kindle Recommendations.) A list offers ebook suggestions, each of which you can mark as "I own it" or "Not interested," or add a 1- to 5-star rating. For deep-tissue adjustments, click the "Fix this" link; the page that appears shows the previous purchases you made that influenced this suggestion. Next to each of these titles you can turn on checkboxes for "This was a gift" and "Don't use for recommendations."

> **TIP** Tucked on the left side of your Amazon-wide Improve Your Recommendations page (that is, the one that controls *all* the suggestions you get), you can turn on a checkbox next to "Show Amazon book recommendations as Kindle editions when possible." Now when you visit Amazon from any computer, the books will be electronic whenever those editions exist.

- **From any web browser.** The Kindle Books section is a pop-up menu away from Amazon's home page. Under the Shop All Departments header, go to Kindle→Kindle Books (or head straight to *http://amzn.to/kfmm105*). The top-level categories alone are enough to keep a taxonomer employed full-time. Way too many to list here, but beyond the obvious (Fiction, Nonfiction, Advice), some groupings that might be worth a quick visit: Free Collections, 100 Books for $3.99 or Less, and the Kindle Daily Deal. Sign up for an email (*http://amzn.to/kfmm108*) to hear about the latter, and you'll get the scoop on some fairly steep discounts on some new title each day.

NOTE It's possible to buy or download free ebooks from a few other sources, though Amazon doesn't do anything to make the process easy. The files must be free from copyright protection and appear in one of the Fire's accepted file formats (.txt, .mobi, and .doc are the most popular; see *http://amzn.to/kfmm133* for the full list). This is great news for fans of Project Gutenberg (*www.gutenberg.org*), the decades-old free ebook repository—not to mention anyone who buys ebooks directly from this book's publisher, O'Reilly Media. As for the hard part: Getting the files onto your Fire is a pain and the books don't even end up in the Books Library. They get shelved in Docs, which is the subject of Chapter 4. That's also where you can learn all about these ebook shuttling maneuvers.

Any books you buy appear in your Fire's Books Library. As with any other Fire media collection, the titles here are divvied up between the ones stored up on Amazon's servers and those you've downloaded to the Fire. Either bucket can be displayed in two ways: as book cover icons on a shelf (Grid view) or as a list of titles and tiny icons (List view). Switch between these two looks by heading to Options bar→Menu and picking the one you want. (One advantage of List view: A percentage indicator shows how far along you are in every title in your collection.)

TIP Comic book fans will definitely want to check out Comixology's free Comics app. These guys have been putting picture/prose mashups on the touchscreen since the iPhone came out. Their catalog is deep (plenty of choices from brands like DC Comics and even a few dozen graphic novels). They've also designed a nifty "guided mode" that pushes to center screen one panel after another, making the print page easier to read on the small screen.

Borrowing and Lending

Many publishers view ebook lending with about as much enthusiasm as they have for video games. Rife with killers and mortal threats, the both of them. And, to be fair, this wariness has a certain logic. If all Kindle owners could borrow as many ebooks as they wanted, why would *anyone* ever buy an ebook? That day will likely never come, thanks to the aforementioned fear. But there are a couple of nascent and fairly useful sharing initiatives available for Fire owners:

- **Loan this title.** You lend out your print books all the time. Why not do the same with your Kindle books? You can...sorta...sometimes. First, the publisher of the book in question needs to deem the title loan-eligible. If that's the case (often it's not), then you can lend the title to a Kindle-using pal for 14 days. During which time, your own access to the book is revoked, and you can only lend each book once. To check whether all these stars align, head over to Amazon.com and drill down to Your Account→Manage Your Kindle→Your Kindle Library. (On the Fire, you can reach the same point by starting from the Kindle Store, tapping the Options bar's Menu icon, and choosing Kindle Account.) Next to each title you've purchased, in the Actions pop-up menu, look for the "Loan this title" option. If it's there, loan away. If it's not, you can't.

- **Kindle Owners Lending Library.** Another hobbled but slightly more interesting program arrived around the time of the Fire's release. Available only to Amazon Prime subscribers (page 88), this program lets you check out one Kindle book per month and keep it as long as you like. On the first day of the next month, you're free to borrow again as long as you've "returned" the book you previously checked out. Onscreen prompts when checking out the new book explain what you need to do. Or do so manually by picking "Return this book" from the Your Kindle Library page mentioned in the previous point. So far, none of the big-name publishers have chosen to participate in this deal, but there are a smattering of *New York Times* bestsellers on the list. To do some virtual borrowing, inside the Fire's Books library, tap Store→Kindle Owners' Lending Library. From the list that appears, click any category (the top one's a catch-all for all eligible books).

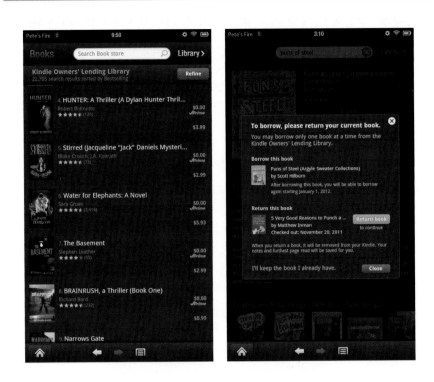

- **Public library ebooks.** Library fans rejoiced when Amazon announced this service. It lets you borrow Kindle-compatible ebooks from more than 11,000 public library websites. You'll need an account to log into your local library's site (which uses a company called Overdrive to participate in the program). Find the book you want, check it out (periods range from 7 to 21 days), and you get whisked off to an Amazon page for the book that lets you decide which Kindle to deliver the book to. After picking your Fire from the "Deliver to" menu, click the "Get library book" button. Back at your Fire, tap Settings→Sync, and the title will be waiting for you in the Device tab of the Books Library.

For now, these perks are just that: frills that might complement your book buying appetite, but won't give you the satisfied feeling you get from an armful of library books.

CHAPTER 3

The Newsstand

AS YOU SAW IN the previous chapter, ebooks look great on the Fire. Later on, you'll learn how movies shrink gracefully from silver- to touchscreen. But magazines and newspapers are a mixed bag. On the one hand, thanks to Amazon's growing clout as an e-power, the company has signed deals with all the biggies: Condé Nast (publisher of *Vanity Fair*, *The New Yorker*, many others), the *New York Times*, *National Geographic*—the list is huge. The heart of the problem: trying to cram a full-sized print page onto a display better suited for books and Angry Birds. The worst offenders are the magazines, most of which don't even try to rejigger their layouts; what you get is a whole lot of panning and zooming.

Most newspapers, to their credit, don't even try this "let's hold our breath and maybe readers won't mind" maneuver. Instead, they ditch all their fancy formatting and deliver plain text plus a few pictures. On an early-generation Kindle—the kind with the black-and-white screen—this formula made sense. It even helped de-gunk ad clutter so readers could focus on articles. But the Fire has illuminated all that's out there on the technicolor Web. It's like being stuck with a radio when all your neighbors have color TVs.

Consider the Newsstand, then, an area where the Fire flickers a bit dimly. To be fair, it's not entirely Amazon's fault. Until periodical publishers redesign their titles for this new screen size, you can either make do with these sub-par pickings, or choose not to. If you're still determined to save some trees and read magazines and newspapers on the Fire, this chapter shows you how to make the most of what's out there.

Apps vs. Kindle Editions

Like any newsstand, the Fire gives you lots of choices. But before grabbing that first pile of magazines, check out the two main format flavors.

- **Apps.** These custom-built readers are designed especially for the Fire. Publishers and their programming teams invest lots of time and money making these things look and work the way they want them to. For example, *The New Yorker* isn't a shrunken snapshot of the print magazine. Instead, designers lay out the whole issue anew to fit your mid-sized screen. They even toss in some digital-only treats: poets reading their work, tappable timelines, hand-crafted typography. Navigation also gets special treatment, giving you app-style freedom to swipe between articles or scroll down a table of contents. This category is filled mainly with titles from magazine moguls Condé Nast and Time, Inc. (*Sports Illustrated*, *People*). Other than that, the pickings are slim.

- **Kindle editions.** Design options here are much more limited. Basically, you can toggle between two views. The first, Page View, shrinks a print magazine replica and stuffs it on your Fire. As mentioned earlier, this approach entails one big tradeoff: lots of panning and zooming to view what was originally meant for a normal-sized print page. Option two—Text View—comes at the problem from a different angle: It strips out all the formatting and leaves you with words plus some oddly positioned graphics. If you believe that half the fun of magazines are those intricate, graphic-heavy layouts, you're in for a letdown. Infographics with their pictures lopped off, for example, are usually just clunky-looking lists. Some Kindle editions, including most newspapers, don't offer Page View; if that's the case you *won't* see the special Page View Enabled note next to the publication's title.

Reading and Navigation

One nice thing about the Kindle edition's design constraints is that all publications that use this format work the same way. Once you understand how to skim pages, browse articles, and flip between Page and Text view, you're set for every periodical that uses this approach. What follows is a quick tour on how to do all that.

> **NOTE** Since every app gets its own design and navigation system, it's tough to offer advice on how to read these things. Sure, the usual "tap the right edge to see the next page" almost always works. But beyond that, different publishers use different designs for the table of contents, skimming pages, and so on. Fortunately, two big software companies power the majority of magazine apps available in these early days of the Fire. Page 67 shows you how they work.

Page View: A Print Magazine Replica

Navigating a magazine in Page View mode gives you a chance to use all your favorite Fire gestures. Tap anywhere on the right edge to turn the page; the left edge flips you back. Swipe in either direction, anywhere on the page, to move forward (right-to-left) or backward (left-to-right). Spread your fingers to zoom in; when zoomed in, pan around by holding and dragging one finger around. Pinch or double-tap to return to normal magnification. Tap the center of the screen to summon the Options bar and up pops a slew of similar choices:

- **Page browser.** A horizontally swipeable carousel of page miniatures, ideal for speedy visual browsing. It's not easy to see details, but usually there's enough to decide whether you want to see what's on that page. To dive in, tap the mini version; tap again on the actual page to dismiss the browser.

- **The page slider.** An even quicker way to zip through the page icons. Hold your finger on its gray, four-ridged tab and move in whichever direction you want to browse. Again, tap any page when you want to pull it up on the big screen.

- **The table of contents.** Represented by the familiar bullet list icon. Tap it for a vertically scrolling list of articles, often divided by publication section. Tap to select an article or tap the bullet list icon again to dismiss it.

- **Search tool.** The magnifier glass in the lower-right corner gets you a top-of-screen search oval and a keyboard. Enter the word or phrase you're looking for, tap the Go button, and a list of results shows up.

Tired of pinching, tapping, and squinting? Toggle over to Text View by tapping the page's center and picking that button in the upper-right corner (if it doesn't show up, it's because a Text View of this page isn't offered, which happens, for example, if the page is an ad).

Text View: Better Text Reading

In this mode, reading newspapers and magazines is much the same as reading ebooks—page 36 in the previous chapter has the full rundown. The short version: Tap the right edge to move forward, the left edge to move back, and the middle of the screen for the Options bar, where you can do things like pick from a table of contents list or adjust font size and background style. One Newsstand-only difference: Middle-screen taps bring up an article navigator; tap either of its arrows (left or right edge) to move between articles in a publication.

Two Ways to Navigate

Two big software companies design the majority of magazine apps you see today: Adobe and WoodWing. Their tools do three things well: accommodate the multimedia additions everyone wants to add; work well with the publisher's existing print operations (still where they earn their bread and butter); and give readers an easy way to navigate these new digital offerings. You won't see either firm's name mentioned anywhere in these apps, but their programming handiwork is what you're using. Here's a quick roundup of the two platforms' key features.

Adobe

Adobe's magazine technology is the choice of high-profile publications like *The New Yorker*, *Wired*, *Vanity Fair*, *Glamour*, *GQ*, *Self*, and *Allure*. Think of the overall layout as a combo vertical and horizontal layout. Swipe left or right to move *between* articles, scroll up and down to peruse an individual piece.

Tap anywhere on the middle of the screen to show the top-row navigation bar. There you'll see three key buttons (left to right): home (an archive page where you can download past issues); a vertical table of contents (a scrollable list of every article in the issue); and a horizontal TOC (a swipeable layout of every article and ad from front page to legalese).

> **TIP** Tap the middle of the screen to summon the page slider (at bottom), and then hold your finger on it and move in either direction to see miniature previews of whatever page you'll land on when you remove your finger.

WoodWing

This firm created the software behind the digital editions of *Sports Illustrated*, *People*, *Time*, *Entertainment Weekly*, and *Real Simple*. Tap anywhere on the *bottom* of the screen to summon a navigation bar. It's similar to the gesture you'd use to get the Fire's ubiquitous Options bar, but rather than touching anywhere in the Fire's middle column, here you need to tap the bottom row. You then get a row of buttons on the lower edge of the screen: Cover, Contents, Page Viewer, and so on. The Contents button gets you a vertically scrollable, hyperlinked list to every item in the issue. Page Viewer produces a row of miniature page snapshots, each of which you can tap to view the page in full.

Touch the middle of any page to dismiss this entire navigational apparatus and use the Fire's swipe left/swipe right gestures to move through the issue page by page. (One common Fire feature that *doesn't* work: tapping in the right or left column to page forward or back—you have to swipe.)

Finally, forget about nap time and multitasking while you're downloading new issues. If your Fire goes to sleep or you switch out of the app and start emailing or browsing the Web, your issue stops mid-stream. Tap the resume arrows on the issue cover to pick up where you left off.

Browsing and Buying

The easiest way to visit the Newsstand is on the Fire itself. On the home screen, tap the Newsstand link, and the screen shows your previously purchased Kindle edition titles. Back issues or purchases you've made online but haven't yet downloaded await in the Cloud tab. Magazine apps get shelved in the App Library.

NOTE You're also free to shop directly on Amazon's website, which also has its own Newsstand section (Amazon.com→ Kindle→Newsstand; *http://amzn.to/kfmm114*). It's useful for impulse buys when you're not near your Fire. Just be sure, on the publication's "Deliver to" menu, to pick your Fire from the device list.

Subscriptions and Digital Editions

I subscribe to the New York Times digital edition. Does that get me the Kindle edition?

Sorry, no. And the *Times* is not alone here. Many publications—including the *New York Review of Books*, *The Atlantic*, and *The Boston Globe*—offer digital subscriptions that don't include separate access to the Kindle version. Particulars vary but one common scenario is what the *Times* does: offer a complex mish-mash of print/app/web access options, none of which get you the Kindle edition. One argument might be: Why would you want it? All three of those versions contain far more content than the Kindle edition. But one nice thing about the Kindle edition is its auto-delivery feature (page 71), which other digital versions usually don't offer. That all said, if you spring for the *Times* Kindle edition, you get a perk on the other side of the fence: free range of the paper's website.

In related news, some magazines give print subscribers their digital edition as a bonus—*The New Yorker*, for one. First, download and then open the app. If you've already registered for access on an app (on an iPad, for example), simply hit the upper-left corner's Sign In button and enter the username and password you previously created. If it's your first time for digital access, you'll need to create an account and then use those credentials to sign in.

To start shopping, tap the Newsstand's upper-right Store link. The scrolling list that appears groups choices by category: Fashion & Entertainment, Sports & Fitness, and so on. To browse magazines or newspapers only, tap those dedicated links on the right side of the page. Filter out sub-categories you don't want, or focus on those you do, by tapping the Refine button. Probably worth noting that, at least in Fire's early days, Amazon still had some categorization issues to work out (two of the bestselling newspapers were...magazines).

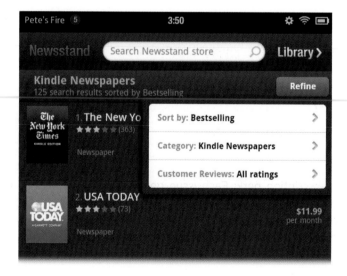

As you poke around, notice how each publication clues you into its format with a tagline: "Magazine – Page View Enabled," "Magazine," and "Newspaper" get you Kindle editions (the latter two versions in Text View only). Any publication tagged as an App is—you guessed it—an app.

Most publications let you either buy single issues or subscriptions. The latter come with 14-day free trials; if you change your mind, head to the Subscription Settings on Amazon.com (Your Account→Manage Your Kindle→Subscription Settings) and, from the Actions menu next to the publication's name, choose "Cancel subscription."

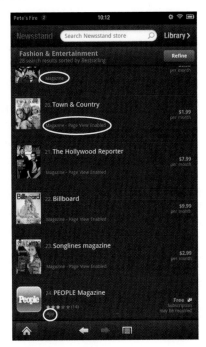

TIP Would you actually answer "yes" to the question "Use name and billing address for marketing purposes?" Well, that's what Amazon's magazine industry dealmakers have chosen for you. It's right there on the Subscription Settings page. You can opt out by clicking "Edit" and, from the pop-up window, turning off the "Name and billing address" checkbox. Leave "E-mail address" unchecked, and then turn on one of the greatest checkbox options ever given to magazine-reading kind: "Use these settings for future newspaper and magazine purchases." Yesssss!

Privacy Settings   ⊠

Allow **Lucky** to use the following information for marketing purposes.

☐ Name and billing address

☐ E-mail address   peter.meyers@gmail.com

Note: It may take up to 60 days for e-mail changes to take effect

☑ Use these settings for future newspaper and magazine purchases.

[Update]   [Cancel]

One nice subscription perk: Each issue gets delivered as soon as it's ready. Imagine waking up at 6:00a.m. and finding your digital copy of *The Beacon-News* loaded up and ready to read. If your Fire isn't in WiFi range, you get the issue the next time you connect.

CHAPTER 4

Documents and Spreadsheets

EVEN BACK IN ITS early, steam-powered days, the Kindle filled students and businesspeople with hope: It could store and display a personal document collection. Fantasies of paper-free days took hold. Amazon helped things along with a clever file shuttling system (via email or USB cable) that assisted transfer chores. Problem was (and remains, for owners of the old school, black-and-white models) those pokey eInk screens. They couldn't handle much more than basic text. And you certainly couldn't edit documents on the Kindle—much less create them from scratch. But the Fire's gorgeous screen and its document-slinging apps have restored hope. Now it's not only *possible* to turn your Kindle into a virtual briefcase, it may become part of your everyday routine.

You have three different ways to get the job done. Each has its own set of pros and cons:

- **The Fire's built-in Docs Library.** Amazon chose to give this tool home-screen billing—and with good reason. It's free, easy to use, and, if all you need to do is tote around and scroll through a PDF or Word file every so often, just right. Load your documents either by email or USB file transfer. Reading works just as it does with Kindle ebooks. If all this sounds good, see the next section for full details.

- **Third-party apps.** Need your mobile reading machine to do more? Perhaps you want to view *and* edit a Word file, tweak that Excel spreadsheet or PowerPoint presentation as you're heading to the big meeting, or add a new chapter to your Lady Gaga vampire novel. Time to enlist the services of a specialized app. Even in the Fire's first week, three of the biggest names in this realm—Documents to Go, Quick Office, and OfficeSuite— had versions up and running. You get all the Docs Library's uploading options, plus the ability to pull from and save to online storage services like Dropbox and Google Docs. You can even install a computer-based utility to keep the Fire's files in sync with, say, your laptop. More info on how to make all this happen on page 78.

- **Web-based tools.** There are a number of competitors in this world (Google Docs, Microsoft's Office 365, Zoho). Each lets you store, compose, and edit Office-like files from just about any web browser...emphasis on "just about." You can get these guys working on the Fire, but the results ain't always pretty. Among the problems you'll encounter are missing menu choices and toolbar buttons (Google Docs) and a crashing web browser (Zoho). Best to wait till these or other developers release apps that show up in Amazon's Android Appstore.

The Built-in Docs Library

Before getting into details of *how* to use Fire's own little library, consider *what* you might want to store here. A typical collection could include recipes, directions, user manuals, long web articles, free ebooks (downloaded from a site like Project Gutenberg; *www.gutenberg.org*). Notice a theme here? Everything's read-only. That is, these are documents you want to peruse but won't need to edit. The Docs viewer is about just that—looking. No copying text, no emailing files. Except for basic note-making and highlighting, the Docs viewer is an eyes-only, hands-off affair.

NOTE   If you spot any similarity between how your files look here and the way Kindle ebooks appear on the Fire, it's because both use much the same internal viewing software.

Adding and Reading Documents

A host of file formats are welcome to this party. From the word processing world, you can open the door for Microsoft Word (.doc and .docx), plain text (.txt), and Rich Text Format (.rtf). Image formats that are okay include the three biggies (JPEG, GIF, and PNG), plus BMP (an old and not very popular option). Ebooks can come dressed in either main Kindle format: MOBI or AZW. Bummer for ebook mavens: EPUB—the most widely used format—is a no-go. You can also send finished web pages (.html or .htm) or, as mentioned earlier, everyone's favorite universal format: the PDF.

NOTE RTF documents, which you can create in Word or any number of other text programs, let you use slightly more complex formatting than plain ol' text files.

Now that you know who's allowed in, here's how to get what you want onto the Fire:

- **By email.** Every Fire gets its own email address. Lonely gadget lovers can use it to send their Fire love notes, but most people will want to send actual files. To see your Fire's unique email address, tap the Docs Library; the address is at the top of the screen. However, no one can send anything to that address without your authorization—not even you. That's how Amazon protects your Fire from spam, should this dedicated email address get into the wrong hands. To register approved senders, go to Personal Document Settings on Amazon.com's Manage Your Kindle page (*http:// amzn.to/kfmm115*). Below the Approved Personal Document E-mail List, click "Add a new approved e-mail address." (You can give the ok-go pass to as many senders as you like.)

Add a new approved e-mail address   ☒

Enter an approved e-mail address.
Tip: Enter a partial address, such as @yourcompany.com, to authorize multiple senders.

E-mail address: [   ]

[Add Address]

Approved Personal Document E-mail List
To prevent spam, your Kindle will only receive files from the following e-mail addresses you have authorized. Learn more

E-mail address	Actions
nobelwinners@sweden.com	Delete
ed.mcmahon@publishersclearinghouse.com	Delete
santa@northpole.com	Delete
richuncle@longlostrelatives.com	Delete
peter.meyers@gmail.com	Delete
Add a new approved e-mail address	

The Personal Docs Settings page is also where you can change the Fire's email address. While you're here, also think about turning on Personal Document Archiving. If you've got other Kindle gadgets or apps, doing so enables you to download your emailed documents to those, too.

Once all that's in place, attach and email your Fire one or more files (up to a max of 25 per email). Then, to receive what you've sent on the Fire, tap the Quick Settings icon (page 22) and hit its Sync button. Give the Fire a minute or three to suck down what you sent it. No individual file can be larger than 50 MB, and you can't email a file to more than 15 Kindles at a time.

TIP A cool experimental feature lets you strip out the formatting from a PDF and end up with plain text only. That way, you can search the text and adjust its font size, for example. Type *Convert* in the subject line of any PDF you send. Converter beware: The results are often messy.

- **From computer to Fire.** The next section has the details on using a USB cable to pipe files from one device to the other.

Looking at what's in your Docs Library is a snap, especially if you've ever read a Kindle ebook. All the same gestures (tap the right margin to turn the page; tap and hold text to add a note or highlight; and so on) all work here. If you need an introduction—or a refresher—pop back to page 36.

TIP Got a file in your Docs Library that you want extra quick access to? On the Docs main screen, tap, hold, and touch any item and then pick "Add to Favorites" from the pop-up menu. Now you've got a home screen shortcut to this file.

Transferring Files from Your Computer

Sideloading is what the geeks call the process of plugging a Fire into a Mac or PC and then siphoning off ebooks, Word files, or PDFs. (The same procedure works for moving photos and home videos, so consider bookmarking this section, even if you don't think you'll use it to move documents.)

Clearly, Amazon doesn't think most folks will ever need to sideload—they don't even include the USB cable you need to make the connection. They will, though, sell you one (here's one well-reviewed model: *http://amzn.to/kfmm135*), so maybe this omission is a way to keep the Fire's price below $200. Whatever your reason, the steps for sending your files sideways go like this:

❶ **Connect the Fire to a computer.** The cable you want is a special flavor of USB: namely, one with a *micro B* plug. That's the same one that comes with recent model Kindles and with other gadgets like BlackBerry phones. Don't mistake this cord with its cousin, the *mini B* USB, which is almost, but not quite, as tiny. Once you've got cable in hand, plug one end into the Fire and the other into a free USB port on your computer. On the Fire, swipe the lock screen's yellow arrow from right to left; a message says you're now free to go ahead and transfer. At the same time, the Fire appears on your desktop (name: KINDLE) or wherever your system puts flash or external drives that you plug in.

❷ **Move files from computer to the Fire.** On the Fire, the folder you're heading for is called Documents. (Following these steps to sideload tunes or visual material? Pick the folder that matches your content: Music, Pictures, and Video.) Drag your files from computer to whichever Fire folder you've just opened.

❸ **Disconnect the Fire.** On the bottom of its screen is a Disconnect button; when you're done with the final transfer, tap it. Now it's safe to unplug the cable from both machines. Power up or wake your Fire as you normally would (page 14) and head to whichever library holds your newly added items; they'll be waiting for you in the Device portion of Docs, Music, and so on.

POWER USERS' NOTE   Plugging in your Fire every time you want to transfer a file can be a pain. Anyone willing to wade through a little app-assisted geekery has two ways around a physical cable link: 1) Make the connection between computer and Fire using WiFi rather than USB, or 2) download a file from a web page (like a Dropbox link or a downloadable ebook file) and then use an app to transfer the file to the Fire's Documents folder. Both procedures are covered in Chapter 6, starting on page 105.

Third-Party Apps

One of the main raps against the Fire is that it's really only good for *consuming* content. Tasks like reading an ebook, watching a TV show, or browsing email make sense on its paperback-sized screen. But are you really going to use its smallish keyboard and display to create anything? If you're like most Fire fans, the answer is probably not. But if you're one of those mobile-loving road warriors, the desire may be there.

To be sure, it's not easy to compose long documents using the three tools—Documents to Go, Quickoffice, and OfficeSuite—profiled in this section. The biggest hindrance is hardware related: The onscreen keyboard doesn't lend itself to tapping out a novel (and you can't attach an external one). But if you've ever wished to leave your five-pound laptop behind for that day trip or overnight, the Fire's first generation of file-editing apps is encouraging news. These three apps can be surprisingly powerful for viewing, editing, sharing, and even creating documents from scratch. Each app may be missing a feature or two, but keep reading, and you're likely to find one that matches your needs.

All three apps handle most Office 101 skills. In the word processing utilities, you get undo/redo; zoomable views (good for increasing onscreen legibility without changing the text's actual font size); bullet and numbered lists; a handful of font choices; and basic styling (italics, bold, paragraph alignment). With spreadsheets, you can create and navigate between multiple worksheets; format cell number style (currency, date, time); pick from a large catalog of ready-to-use functions (AVERAGE, COUNTIF, LOOKUP); and add rows and columns. The PowerPoint stand-ins are the most limited, at least in terms of features shared by all three apps. Every one in the trio lets you view presentations made on a computer, but don't count on extremely sophisticated formatting, and builds and transitions don't show up on the small screen.

Opening and emailing files work much the same way in all three apps, too. You can email files to yourself and then, in whichever app you use for that task, tap the message's Open button and pick the Office-viewing app you want to use to open the attachment. If you transfer a file from your computer to your Fire (as described on page 105), you need only to navigate in the Office-viewing app to whichever folder you stashed your file in. To move files in the *other* direction—that is, email them off your Fire—simply add an attachment in your email app of choice; a pop-up menu lets you pick the file.

On the other hand, the apps vary greatly in their willingness to interact with online storage services like Google Docs and Dropbox. So-called Cloud-based offerings like these can be supremely useful for big travelers and those who move between multiple computers, smartphones, and tablets. You never have to worry about where the latest version is—it's always stored online.

One final similarity worth mentioning: All three apps come in cheap (sometimes free) and expensive versions. The cheap kind gets you the ability to view, but not create or edit, a file. For that, you need to pony up for the more expensive edition.

Documents to Go

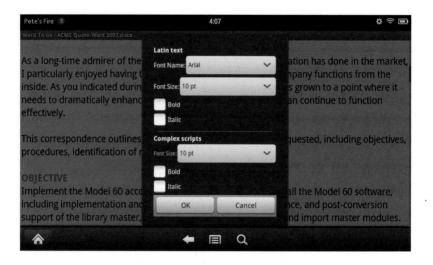

Documents to Go's big advantage is its unique desktop companion software. Install the free utility on a regular computer—Windows-only, alas—and you're a sync-button push away from mirror-image files on both your Fire and any of your regular computers. But an even bigger draw is how simple and intuitive this app is. Pretty much every icon and menu choice is dead simple to discern and operate. For an app that you may dip into every couple of weeks, not having to pause and figure things out is probably worth the price of admission.

That's not to say Documents to Go is underpowered. It meets most needs, starting with the ability to create, edit, and view Word, Excel, and PowerPoint files (both the previous generation file types—.doc, .xls, .ppt—and the newer editions with an "x" at the end of their file extensions). A PDF reader is also part of the lineup. Other special talents worth noting: In Word you can create and view others' comments, modify line spacing, create tables, and view word count. You can also tap into any files you've stored up in Google Docs—and create new ones on the Fire.

Quickoffice

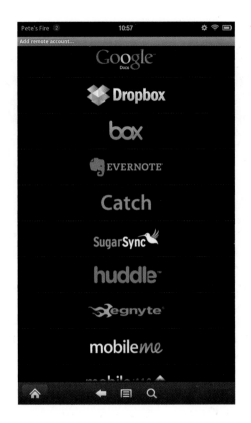

Quickoffice Pro earns an "A" for "works and plays well with others." It's a snap to tap into online file storage services like Google Docs, Dropbox, Box.net, SugarSync—the list goes on. So if you're into this increasingly popular method of file storage and sharing, you may have found your match. Another, slightly more quirky perk: *text recital*, which does just what it suggests, using a slightly grating computer voice to read a document aloud.

A powerful find-and-replace tool (in Word and Excel) is a nice helper. Quickoffice's PowerPoint design skills are also top-notch. (Though, again, reality check time: No transitions or builds will show up on the small screen.) You get more slide design tools than the other two apps, including ready-to-use templates for page layouts like "Picture with Caption" and Title Only, and you can also include circles, arrows, and lines. One downside: Many of the toolbar icons don't look much like their underlying tool—and they have no identifying text labels. If you don't use the app frequently, you may get frustrated relearning the toolbar each time.

OfficeSuite

This app is the best option for Excel jockeys. You get a full complement of chart-creating tools (column, bar, pie, and area) and smoothest-in-class speed for switching between worksheets. PowerPoint's not too shabby either. Notes are visible if you want 'em, and a play button lets you put the slides on auto-advance (Quickoffice has that feature, too). If you need to create a slideshow on your Fire, you can pick from 10 templates, as well as background art. Nothing fancy, but these visuals may make you appear more prepared. What OfficeSuite lacks, though, may be a dealbreaker: It has no integration at all with any of the online storage services.

PART II

Watching and Listening

CHAPTER **5**

Watching TV and Movies

IF YOU'VE GOT A kid or commute in your life, you'll *love* the Fire's talents as a video jukebox. With its growing lineup of mainstream TV shows and movies, Amazon is giving Netflix and Apple a reason to look over their shoulders. It's all part of Jeff Bezos's master plan to turn what began as his online bookselling site into something much bigger. He's also fixing to put the competitive scare into your local cable company. Consider, for example, what's playing on your local Fireplex:

- **TV shows.** Networks big and small have signed on—everyone from ABC to VH1, and most of the alphabet in between. BBC, CBS, and Comedy Central are among those who've licensed at least a decent chunk of their catalog. All told, you have about 8,000 shows to pick from, most of which you can buy; some are available for rent.

- **Movies.** The lineup here is much bigger—you can choose from about 45,000 flicks. Sure, some are straight from the discount bin, but there are also plenty of A-list options featuring big name stars and directors. Rent or buy, the choice is yours.

- **Prime Instant Videos.** Here's where Amazon gets really clever. Subscribing to the $79-a-year free-shipping service (page 88) gets you unlimited, commercial-free access to a library of 10,000-plus TV shows and movies. Everything here gets streamed. You can't download any of these files, so it's not a substitute for the in-flight movie. But it's a huge addition to your living room lineup.

This last category may turn out to be Amazon's biggest lure—especially for those thinking about signing up for (or renewing) a Netflix subscription. It may even siphon off a million or so potential iPad buyers, thanks to how it stocks any Fire with an incredibly large collection of things to watch. Add in the free shipping that made Amazon Prime famous, and the ever-increasing number of perks like one ebook-a-month borrowing (page 59), and you can see why this show is starting to attract a crowd.

NOTE Since mid-2011, Amazon has been aggressively inking deals to bulk up its video catalog. By the time you read this page, the actual number of titles available will surely be larger than what's listed above. Check *http://amzn.to/kfmm117* for the latest lineup.

Now Playing on Amazon Prime: TV Shows, Movies, Ebooks

One way to get lots of stuff on your Fire requires no uploading whatsoever. Amazon's $79 per year Prime service is slowly but surely turning from a free shipping proposition—all-you-can-order, two-day deliveries—into a fairly well stocked media buffet bar. In the months leading up to the Fire's release, Amazon added a few sweeteners, aimed especially at its new tablet owners. Most attractive is the Prime Instant Video service—the heart of the deal is that Prime subscribers get streaming access to a growing library of 10,000-plus TV shows and movies. None of these movies are the latest releases, but there's enough that you'll likely find something worth watching. Another new Prime subscriber benefit: ebook library lending. Once a month

you get to pick from a small but decent list of lendable ebooks. Keep each one for as long as you like, and 30 days later you're free to check out a new title (see page 60 for the full scoop). Amazon's hoping to lure at least a few Fire fence-sitters by tossing in a month of Prime for free to any new device owner. Quick caveat for Prime veterans: These perks only go to those individuals who fork over the $79 annual fee. That means anyone who enjoys free Prime shipping thanks to programs like Amazon Mom, Amazon Student, or even because they live under the same roof as a paying Prime member—all those folks are out of luck. No Prime media freebies for their Fire unless they pay their own $79.

Browsing and Downloading

Finding something to watch on your Fire is probably *easier* than navigating that 500-channel gridlock most TVs confront you with. On the Fire's home screen, tap the Video Library and, if it's not yet selected, head into the upper-right Store link. Here you see the three big buckets described at the top of the chapter—Prime Instant Videos, Movies, TV Shows. (Can you tell which one Amazon's pushing?)

Each of these buckets gets its own horizontally swipeable row and a "View all" link for deep dives. On the "View all" screen, the listings are chunked into categories to make it easier to find the type of thing you feel like watching. If you're in TV-land, for example, you get top-level sections for Popular TV Shows, Latest TV Episodes, Editor's Picks, All Genres, and so on. The choices here vary based on whether you're looking at movies or TV shows. Most of these sections are self-explanatory, but four in particular are worth paying a regular visit to:

TIP Show or hide Prime choices by toggling between those two adjacent tabs—Prime and All—on the top of most higher level browsing pages in the Store. Tap Prime, for example, and the only thing you'll see are Prime freebies.

Swipe right to left
for more choices

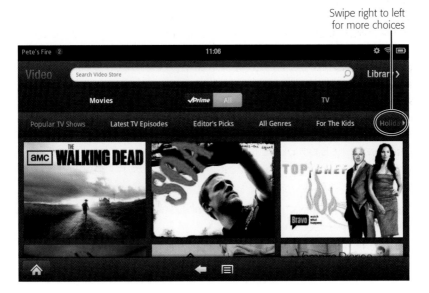

- **New Releases.** You won't get what's opening at your local cinema this weekend, of course. But this section is a reliable way to track what's emerging from Hollywood's staggered release chute (theaters, DVD releases, cable, and so on).

TIP Another way to keep an eye on this hard-to-track radar: Sign up for one of the periodic newsletters that Amazon sends out. Head to Amazon.com's Communications page (open the Your Account link using any web browser and, in the Settings section, choose "E-mail Preferences & Notifications"). Then sign up for the weekly Movies & TV email to hear about new releases.

- **Editor's Picks.** This one's fun if for no other reason than checking out the zany groupings that someone at Amazon HQ has concocted: Built-in Babysitter, Canceled Too Soon, To Boldly Go (more than just *Star Trek*—sci-fi fringe fare like *Firefly*, *Farscape*, and the criminally underrated, Emmy-award winning *Red Dwarf*).

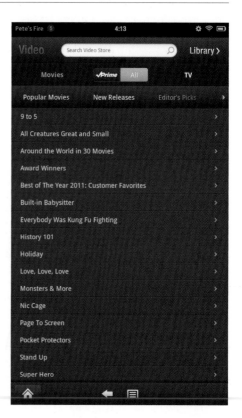

- **All Genres.** Head here if you want to browse the aisles at your own pace as you did during Blockbuster's better days. When you tap this option, further choices appear for Action & Adventure, Comedy, Documentary, Drama, Foreign Films, and Sci-Fi & Fantasy.

- **Deals.** Worried about all the money you're spending filling up your bargain-priced Fire? Here's a place to sort through just the $1.99 and $2.99 movie rentals, and, among the TV shows, the 99-centers, and free TV extras (typically, pre-season sneak peaks).

Finally, if you've got a particular title in mind, forget all this swiping and tapping. Head to the screen-top search oval and tap to summon the keyboard. Begin entering what you're looking for and, as you type, a list of suggestions appears in a list below the oval. The choices here adjust on-the-fly; as you enter more letters, the list shrinks to reflect what you've entered. *Di*, for example, gets you a dozen or so choices including *Dick Van Dyke*, *Diary of a Wimpy Kid*, and *Diego* (yep, the search tool includes actors, movies, and TV shows alike). Add a letter or two—say, *Dica*—and now you're looking at only *Dica* and *DiCaprio* (the first entry simply reflects what you've typed; the second is—well, you know who he is). Tap to pick whichever suggestion you want or hit the keyboard's Search button to search for exactly what you've entered.

TIP Did you know that with these suggestion-powered search ovals—on Amazon, Google, or pretty much anywhere else—you don't *have* to pick one of the auto-suggest options? Perhaps you're searching for something extraordinarily rare, something that no one else has entered before. (After all, that's how these lists are created. They simply draw from what others have previously searched for.) If you don't like the choices on the list, just keep typing.

Buying and Renting Options

Once you've found something that looks good, tap its title-card icon. The page you arrive at is filled with extra info like a synopsis, show details (cast, director, length), and a row of "Customers who bought this item also bought" suggestions. (If you tap a TV show, your first stop is a list of episodes; tap any one of these to get to the individual show page.)

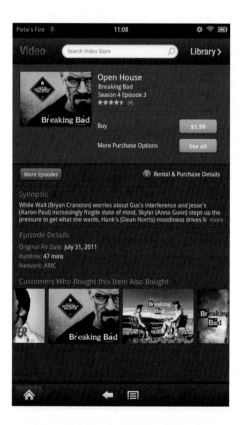

TIP If an actor's name is listed in orange, that means it's tap-linked to other productions available on Amazon.

You'll also see one or more buttons with your buying and rental options. Truth be told, while you'll run into *many* pricing variations, most of your options have already been decided for you. Some TV shows you can rent; most you can buy. Some shows let you grab the full season; others only offer individual episodes. But as far as actual decision making goes, your work mainly boils down to: finding what you want and then deciding whether to get the HD version or the lower-quality standard definition (see the following Note for help choosing).

And even that's not always an option. Bottom line: If you're looking to write a market research report or an, uh, advice book, the minutiae of subtle differences in this realm is maddening. But if you're just a regular Fire owner looking for something to watch, your decision should be pretty simple. Ahead, an overview of the range of pricing and availability options in both TV and movies.

NOTE Is it worth ponying up for HD? Well, you won't be able to watch, or even download, the HD version on your Fire; instead, you'll get the standard-def version. But this being the land of clouds and syncing, when you do get back to your Amazon-compatible HDTV (full details on page 101), there you can watch the extreme def in its full glory.

TV Shows

The range of prices, and rent vs. buy options, is relatively consistent here, at least compared to the Wild West of online movies. Most shows are available for purchase only, although a few let you rent episodes. Single episodes cost a buck or two for standard definition; usually $3 for HD. The prices of full-season packages vary widely based on how many episodes there are and which quality you pick. Any show that's part of the Prime Instant Video package is free to Prime subscribers, who see a nice trio of zeroes next to its name.

NOTE Some shows list seasons that, frustratingly, aren't available. The clue? There's no button next to each individual episode's title (for example: *Survivor, season 12*).

Movies

Simply put, the different pricing tiers, rental duration periods, and you-can-buy-but-you-can't-rent restrictions here are *insane.* Imagine, for example, randomly picking seven different movies to get a general sense of how much things cost, what's for rent, what's for sale, and so on. Now imagine that each title were priced differently and were available for different periods of time. (Actually, you don't have to imagine, because that's the case for these films: *Super 8*, *Spy Kid 4*, *Winnie the Pooh*, *Cars 2*, *Toy Story*, *The Lion King*, and *Horrible Bosses*.) Pity the Amazon accountants who have to track all this stuff!

Fortunately, none of this really matters to you, Fire owner. All you need to do is find what you want and then decide whether any of its pricing packages match what you're prepared to spend. Rentals range from one to three days and cost between a buck and $5. HD costs more, standard definition costs less. To buy will cost you between $5 and $15.

Got it? Now, go get it.

Downloading and Playing

To buy something, tap the button of the same name. The Fire then asks you to confirm your intent to purchase, at which point you get two buttons: Watch Now and Download. The first lets you stream the show to the Fire, which offers the advantage of not occupying any of your Fire's limited storage space. Streaming does, however, require a working WiFi connection; the video starts about 10 seconds after you tap the button.

Go for the Download button if you'll be out of WiFi range. Once tapped, this button sprouts a little Options button, which you can use to pause or cancel the download. Full downloads vary widely in time, depending on the speed of your Internet connection and the length of what you're downloading.

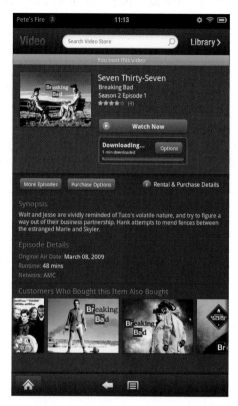

TIP Actually playing a downloaded video isn't always as one-tap-simple as you might expect. If you decide immediately after buying to play it, tap the Watch Now button on its purchase page. If you wait till later and navigate to Video→Device and then tap it, the show doesn't start right away. Instead, you're taken back to the video store and, if it's a TV show, dumped on the season page it came from. Now you need to scroll down and find the episode you bought—you'll see a white, downward-pointing arrow to the right of its title. Here's where you can tap to play. Movies work the same way, except you're taken to a dedicated viewing screen. Tap the Watch Now button to start.

Renting works similarly. Tap the orange button with the price; it turns green and says Rent. Tap again, and you see the Watch Now and Download buttons. If you tap the latter, you get a warning that your rental period is about to start (see the box on page 95 for the legal nitty gritty). If you go ahead and tap Download, that button is replaced by a progress indicator and a small Options button, same as you see when buying a video. Tap that and, from a pop-up menu, you can either pause or cancel the download.

Many titles sport a "See all" button next to More Purchase Options. Tap it, and a pop-up window gives you whatever choices are available—to buy, regular rental, HD rental, and so on. After you make your choice, the window asks you to confirm your purchase. Now you're back facing the options already described: two buttons, one saying Watch Now, the other saying Download. If you tap Download, you get a pop-up window notifying you that you're about to start the 48-hour (or however long) rental period. And it also reminds you that "you can download this video to only one device but you can stream to multiple devices" as described in the box below.

TIP Want to skip ahead while watching any video? Tap anywhere on the screen to display the player controls and then hold and drag your finger along the progress bar. Stop wherever you want and lift your finger off the screen when you're ready to watch.

MESSAGE FROM THE LAWYERS

Your TV and Movie Viewing Rights

As you've probably noticed, when it comes to deals made between Amazon and the TV and movie studios, the word "simple" rarely enters the conversation. You can tell by the wide variation in prices and rental times on the site's video catalog pages. If the label next to the button says "48 Hour Rental," there's your answer for how long you can keep it. Then there's the matter of the fine print waiting behind the "Rental & Purchase Details" link (also found on the same screen as the buying and rental buttons). Here's a briefing for all non-lawyers out there:

- **Rentals.** Once you hand over your money, you get a 30-day window during which you can watch the movie. The stopwatch begins—for 24 hours, 48 hours, or however long your video's rental button says—the moment you tap either the Watch Now or Download button. You can watch the show on multiple devices (your Fire, your PC, your big-screen TV), but you face a few restrictions. If you stream it (by tapping the Watch Now button), you can only do so to one device at a time. You can, of course, stream the first half to your Fire and then watch the second half on your TV—that's the whole point of Whispersync, as explained on page 101. If you download the video to your Fire, you can't download it to another device, but you can stream it to a non-Fire device.

- **Purchases.** In most cases, you're free to watch any video you buy as many times as you like. One caveat: You can watch on Amazon-approved hardware only, like the Fire, your computer, or the living room gadgets listed at *http://amzn.to/kfmm119*. And you definitely won't find any iGadget made by Apple on this list. If you don't want to download a purchase to your Fire and prefer instead to stream it, here's the deal: You can't stream the video to *another* device while you're streaming to your Fire. And if you do want to download it, you can only do so to two devices at a time. So if you've downloaded a flick to your Fire and PC and now want it on your TV, remove it from tablet or computer first. On the Fire, just tap, hold, and select Delete Download.

App Spotlight: Netflix and Hulu

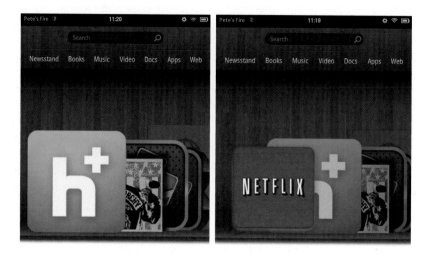

Amazon, of course, isn't the only show in town. Both Netflix and Hulu have joined the fun with Fire-friendly apps. Each of these streaming media services have fairly substantial catalogs. Netflix is best for movie lovers, while Hulu specializes in TV. (Both, however, offer plenty of titles from big and small screen entertainers alike.)

Is it worth signing up for either—or both? That's a tough one to answer, given everyone's different viewing tastes. Plus, both Hulu's and Netflix's lineups overlap quite a bit with each other and with Amazon's listings. It'd take something like an exhaustively researched table to even begin to outline the differences. Well, whaddya know? The good people over at paidContent.org have done just that. Check out their findings: *http://bit.ly/kfmm109*. If you're still game to use these apps, here's a quick tour of what you'll find and how things work.

> **NOTE** Both services are app-only affairs. You can't watch the goodies on either site using the Fire's web browser. Both also offer free trial accounts. You can find more info on signup and lineup at *www.netflix.com* and *www.hulu.com*.

Netflix

The app is free to download from Amazon's Appstore (page 28), but you'll need a Netflix account to actually watch anything. Plans start at $8 per month. After opening the app, log in using your Netflix name and password. The opening screen puts your two main finding methods in front of you:

- **The main grid.** This is Netflix's best effort to whet your whistle. You can swipe each row horizontally to explore it, and scroll vertically to see more categories. In other words, scroll down through categories like Instant Queue (more on that in a moment), "Steamy Romantic Movies based on a book," "Dark TV Shows," and so on, and then swipe across when you want to explore more than the three or so titles that appear at a time. You'll also see rows custom built around what Netflix's software predictors think you'll like: "Top 10 for Tom." Finally, don't miss the groupings that Netflix builds around what you've recently watched. For example: "Like: *Life in a Day*."

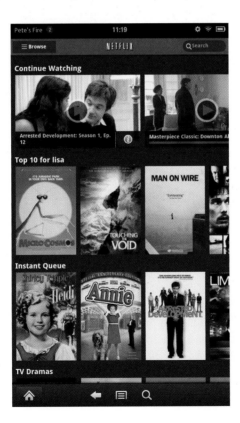

- **The Browse button.** Tapping this upper-left button pops up a list of categories you can explore—everything from Anime to Sci-Fi & Fantasy. Tap any of these, and the home page's grid gets broken up into sub-categories. Enter Children & Family, for example, and you get: Suggestions for You, New Arrivals, Ages 0-2, and so on.

> **NOTE** There's also the search oval. It works just as you'd expect. Tap to summon the keyboard and enter what you're looking for.

Don't miss the Instant Queue, which lets you build a list of want-to-watch faves as you browse. You can add to it on Netflix's website or in the app. Tap or click a movie's Add to Instant Queue button, and this ever-updating playlist is waiting for you on the app's home screen.

To play something now, tap its title card. On the detail window that pops up, tap the red Play button on the cover art (or add it to your Instant Queue for watching later). Once the flick begins, tap the screen once at any time to summon the progress slider. Tap, hold, and slide it to move to a different point, or just tap wherever you want to go to.

To adjust volume, use the Fire's built-in controller, which you can find by tapping the screen once and then tapping again the Quick Settings icon (page 22). Some titles have non-English dialogue available; tap the speech bubble on the right side of the progress slider, and a pop-up window lets you know whether options exist. In the same spot, you can turn on subtitles if they're available.

Netflix is best known for movies, but they also have a decent TV show catalog. Explore via the Browse button—TV Shows is the first genre listed. Tap that, and you get a new main screen grid with suggestions, new arrivals, and lots of specific sub-categories (British TV Shows, Classic TV). If the show's got multiple seasons, when you tap its title card, you get a drop-down menu that you can pick from. Play any episode below that by clicking the red Play arrow to the far right of each title.

> **TIP** If you can't quite reach the final episode in a season, it's probably because your Fire's in landscape orientation. Switch to portrait, and it wiggles onto the bottom of the list.

Hulu Plus

It'll cost ya 8 bucks a month to watch most of this service's TV shows and movies, but, unlike Netflix, the app does offer a few freebies for non-payers. Emphasis on a *few*. To see them, launch the app and tap the Free Gallery icon. There you'll find about a dozen TV episodes, plus a movie or two. If you do want to sign up for the real deal, do so from a real computer if you can, since the Fire doesn't get along particularly well with Hulu's website. Return to the app and tap on any title not in the Free Gallery. A pop-up window asks you to enter your user name and password.

> **TIP** If you're on the Fire and encounter a *second* log-in page, looking like it's been pulled from the Web, blow right by it by tapping the upper-right corner Done button.

To find something to watch, tap on either of the ubiquitous TV or Movies icons. Pick TV, for example, and you get a vertically scrolling list of different shows. The top-left drop-down menu is your main filtering option—it's where you decide how the list of shows gets organized: Featured, Most Popular, Recently Added, Alphabetical, and Networks. The latter gets you a new page dedicated to each of the dozens of individual networks that Hulu has deals with.

Also on the main TV page is an upper-right drop-down menu for picking between episodes (full shows) and clips (short snippets like SNL sketches). On the Movies page, the same menu offers full movies or trailers. Tucked nearby is a magnifying-glass icon for search. When you find something you like, tap the show's title to start playing it or use the right-side exposure triangle to get a menu that lets you add the show to your queue (a playlist of to-watch items) or get more info (synopsis, cast). Build a queue by tapping the button of the same name below any show or movie.

Once you've got something playing, tap the screen to summon the bottom-of-the-screen progress bar. Then you can tap and hold anywhere to see the time spot you'll jump to if you release your finger. Drag to a different position if you want to go somewhere else, or drag up and off the bar to stay where you are.

Hulu does have one big annoyance: Ads are a big part of the lineup. Even for paying customers, they show up frequently. Switch around between TV shows, and before each one plays you get to watch the same ad you just saw the last time you channel surfed. Gets old, quickly.

Syncing and Sharing

Sorry, you can't share your shows and flicks—at least not in the same way you lend print books and DVDs. Instead, Amazon provides Fire owners with a video-friendly version of its Whispersync service (page 101). Start watching *Top Chef* on the train home, for example, and you can then pick up where you left off on the big screen.

Before you get too excited, though, know that this undertaking takes a bit of work to set up. But here's one big reason to read on: You need to follow these same steps to get your Amazon videos from small to big screen (that is, from your Fire onto your boob tube), so it's a good way to beef up your living room lineup. To Amazon's credit, they've done deals with almost a dozen big-name consumer electronics companies (including Sony, Samsung, and TiVo). If you've got a relatively recent model HDTV, Blu-ray player, DVR, or media-streaming device, there's a decent chance you can use it for your Amazon video downloads.

Start by heading to *http://amzn.to/kfmm119* to see if your device is listed. If so, click Register and then follow the instructions for your unit. Next, buy or rent the video you want (use your Fire or shop on the Web from a regular computer). To get the video onto your TV, go to Amazon.com→Amazon Instant Video→Your Video Library (*http://amzn.to/kfmm121*). Click to open the show you want. Expand the plus (+) button next to the show's name and then click the same button next to Download; choose the device you just registered. The next time your TV or DVR syncs, the download begins.

Having done all that, the video-friendly Whispersync feature now knows where you start and stop, and makes the switching between devices seamless—usually. Some devices don't cooperate (the TiVo Premiere, for example). The manual workaround is less sexy but fairly simple. Assuming you're shifting from Fire to living room TV, take note of the time marker on your Fire-watched show (tap the screen to see the progress slider). On the big screen, fast forward till you get close to that point. Kick off your shoes, press Play, and be thankful you're not an Amazon engineer.

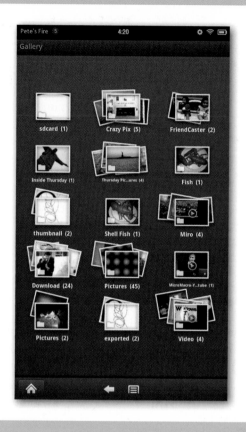

Gallery

sdcard (1)   Crazy Pix (5)   FriendCaster (2)

Inside Thursday (1)   Thursday Pic...ures (4)   Fish (1)

thumbnail (2)   Shell Fish (1)   Miro (4)

Download (24)   Pictures (45)   MicroMacro-Y...tube (1)

Pictures (2)   exported (2)   Video (4)

CHAPTER 6

Photos and Home Videos

EVER SEE A KID these days swipe a photo on a laptop screen? When the thing doesn't budge, the ensuing look—part puzzled, part frustrated—says it all. Pictures in the Touchscreen Age were meant to be swiped, pinched, and tapped. It's just so darn fun zooming in and out and flicking across huge collections. Is it really a surprise that we rarely bother rummaging through photo-filled shoeboxes anymore?

For its part, the Fire makes picture browsing lots of fun. Thanks to a built-in Amazon app called Gallery, your Fire is ready to serve as a portable memory machine—a showcase for the best pictures (and videos) in your collection. This chapter puts it all into focus: from moving your memories onto the Fire, getting (and keeping) them organized, and sharing and showing 'em off.

Getting Pictures and Videos onto the Fire

Three different approaches await for when you're ready to transfer images to the Fire. All three methods are worth knowing about, but the one you'll want depends on how much you're moving. Email is best for small batch transfers; PC-to-Fire connections work well for a few dozen pics, or even slightly larger collections; and a dedicated, web-syncing app is what you need to handle large and constantly changing photo galleries.

NOTE If you've uploaded photos or videos to Amazon's Cloud Drive (page 31), you may be wondering whether there's an easy route between those collections and the Fire. Well, there isn't, at least not as of this writing (though you can be sure that feature is on some Seattle engineer's to do list). Fact is, for now, you can't even use the Fire's web browser to surf over to those images and download them.

Email to Your Fire

Got just a few photos, or a couple videos, you want to pop onto the Fire? Email 'em. Whether you use the Fire's built-in email app (page 147) or a third-party alternative, the benefit of this route is its simplicity. When you open the email on the Fire, simply save the attachments to the Gallery app. This method is great for when your spouse forwards an adorable kid photo, you snap a showstopper on your cellphone, or you're about to head to Home Depot for a sink faucet replacement.

Fire's official emailer gives you two viewing options at the bottom of any image-bearing message: Open and Save. The first lets you see the image directly in the email, the second shuttles things over to the Gallery app and sticks them in a photo stack called Download. Page 114 has details on the Gallery's inner workings.

USB Cable and WiFi Transfers

For big batch transfers, email is slow...like filling up a pasta pot using a table-spoon. The best method for multi-picture loads is via cable. You'll need one of the Fire-friendly "micro B" USB variety (page 78). Hook it up to any computer and you can move hundreds of pictures and videos in a matter of minutes. Page 78 guides you through the process.

Sometimes, though, you don't have a cable handy. Or perhaps your computer's USB ports are all occupied. With the help of a handy app called WiFi File Explorer PRO, neither is a real obstacle. This app creates a virtual WiFi bridge between computer and Fire. Use it to move as many files as you like, as often as you want. Once you've downloaded the $0.99 app from the Appstore (instructions on how to do that begin on page 28), the following steps explain how to put it to work.

> **NOTE** Why would you ever go the wired route when you've got this cordless alternative? USB's quicker, for one, which can make a difference if you're moving a lot of stuff. And, as you'll see in the following steps, the WiFi File Explorer app gets just a tad geeky. Technophobes may not want to get unplugged.

❶ **On your Fire, launch WiFi File Explorer.** The first screen you see lists the WiFi network you're on. The blue box below that name starts off saying "Starting..." and changes to "Serving..." a few seconds later, when the computer and Fire see each other. A message window pops up listing one key bit of info you'll need in a moment—the web address of your newly WiFi-connected Fire. Write that down (including the *http://* part) and then tap the window's Done button.

Transcribing the web address is a pain, but you can avoid writing it down by emailing it to yourself. Simply tap the @ sign icon to the right of where it says File Explorer Web URL. Once you've finished the next step, save yourself even more time by saving it as a bookmark in your web browser. (For this step to work, you need to have at least one email app up and running; Chapter 8 helps you make that happen.)

❷ **On your computer, open a web browser and enter that web address.** The page that appears is a folder-by-folder listing of everything that's on your Fire. Unless you're a certified computer science jockey, don't futz around with anything you see here. You probably know this, but it's worth pointing out: Willy-nilly deletions are a quick way to turn your Fire into a 14-ounce paperweight. Stick with the instructions ahead, and you'll do no harm.

❸ **Open either the Pictures or the Video folder.** The folder you open is the folder you'll transfer files *into*. That's important because later on, back on your Fire, the Gallery app organizes its contents into folder-style stacks. So you want, for example, all your photos to be in the Pictures folder, all your home movies to be in the Video folder, and so on.

In your web browser, you may need to scroll down a bit to see the folder you want. Double-click the folder's name to open it. Now you see all the files in whichever folder you clicked.

❹ Pick the files on your computer you want to transfer. You need to knock
out two tasks here: First, click Select File (lower-right corner) to open a
file-browsing window on your computer. From there, navigate to where you
store your photos or movies. To select more than one file at a time, press
Ctrl (⌘ on a Mac) as you click each file's name. Click Open when you've
picked everything you want.

Second, click Upload Files (turn on the Overwrite checkbox if you're replac-
ing a file that's currently on your Fire). A progress bar replaces the Upload
Files button and shows how quickly things are moving.

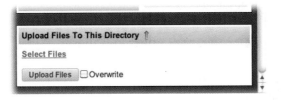

To transfer more files—from another folder on your computer, or to pick a
few home movies if you initially moved over pictures—make sure you're in
the appropriate folder. Use the folder list at the top of the window (where
it says */mnt/sdcard/*) to navigate between folders. For example, to move
from Pictures to Video, click *sdcard/* and, on the page that appears, navigate down to and click Video.

❺ Close the web browser window and the WiFi File Explorer app. Close the
window just as you would any other web page (don't hide or minimize it—
choose File→Close Window, or whatever choice your browser offers). On
your Fire, tap the Option bar's menu icon and then choose Exit.

Whatever you've moved over is now ready for viewing in the Gallery app. (Page
114 has the scoop on how to look and move around there.)

File format-compatibility is a bugaboo for any home video veteran. What plays on one gadget or operating system doesn't always work on another. Among the Fire-friendly formats are: .mp4, .3gp, and .webm. Unfortunately for veterans of format wars past, .mpeg, .mov, .avi and .wmv *didn't* make the cut. (You can find the full list of Fire-friendly video file types at *http://amzn.to/kfmm137*.) If you've got some converting to do, Handbrake (*http://bit.ly/kfmm139*) is a free Windows- and Mac-compatible tool that, while slightly geeky, can help tackle most conversion projects. Miro Video Converter (Mac-only, free; *www.mirovideoconverter.com*) and DVD Catalyst 4 (Windows, $10; *http://bit.ly/kfmm141*) also get high marks from those who've used them.

Creating and Organizing Folders in Gallery

How do you keep what's inside your Gallery organized? The Fire starts you off with two basic groups—Pictures and Video—each of which gets its own stacked image pile. But someday you may want to impose a little order. Perhaps you want to sub-divide your photos into related groups (Kids, Pets). Or maybe you haven't even done anything yet, and you're starting to see image stacks appear with oddball names like *sdcard (1)* and *Download (24)*. What the?

To be frank, Amazon didn't apply a whole lotta programming polish to this particular corner of the device. Is it fun and easy to swipe through any pix you move into the Pictures folder? Absolutely. Does the device make it simple to organize that collection? Nope. Here's how to combat the clutter.

- **Do nothing.** This method has the enormous and obvious advantage of requiring no additional work. The main tradeoff is that

your Gallery can start resembling those old photo-filled shoeboxes, with everything flopping around pell mell. Finding things can require a lot of flicking. It doesn't help that the Gallery groups pictures according to the date you imported the files—even when the photos themselves carry the correct *older* date info. So if you import a bunch of pix from 2001, 2003, and 2005, you won't get three neat yearly stacks when you tap the Organize By Date icon (page 114). Who's idea was *that*? Surely that bug will be fixed at some point. Compounding the problem: Other image-generating apps don't always behave the way you want them to. In SketchBook Mobile (page 213), for example, when you export an image, it creates two new folders called *exported* and *thumbnail* and puts copies (big and small, respectively) of your art in both locations.

–continued–

- **Organize from your computer.** Your first step is to connect the Fire to your Mac or Windows machine, as described on page 78. The Fire appears like any other external hard drive, and you're free to navigate its various folders: Books, Documents, Pictures, and so on. Here's where you can really roll up your sleeves and stick things where you want. Inside the Pictures folder you might want to create subfolders for Kids and Pets. Once you disconnect and launch the Gallery, you may notice one puzzling thing right away. Those two new subfolders aren't *inside* the Pictures folder—they're at the same level. That's one of Fire's quirky organizational rules. In the Gallery, every folder you create on the Fire when it's mounted on your computer appears as its own image stack. So no matter where you create new folders—inside other existing folders, at the same level as Pictures and Videos, wherever—what you'll see inside the Gallery are image stacks, one for each folder.

- **Organize using an app.** As with transferring files, the advantage here is you don't have to mess with a USB cable. Use an app like WiFi File Explorer, which lets you create new folders on the Fire once you've launched a view of the device's contents in your computer's web browser (page 105). Or, for even more power, try an app like ES File Explorer; it lets you burrow seriously deep into your Fire's innards and do things like move files between folders. But beware that with convenience (namely, of not having to manually connect using a USB cable) comes responsibility. The Fire doesn't always like having these apps reapportion and add to its innards.

  If you notice anything funky or sluggish, the best thing to do is quit the app you're using and restart the Fire.

Photo- and Video-viewing Apps

All this file transferring and organizing....who needs it? Perhaps you're thinking: "Hey, I've already paid my dues to Picasa (...Flickr...Facebook). Do I really have to go through the agony of uploading and organizing *again*? Isn't there an easy way to view images on the sites I already use?"

Thank heavens, there is.

Millions of people today already post their favorite photos and videos online. Recognizing this, a few savvy app makers have released tools for tapping into, browsing, and sharing these collections directly from the Fire. If you've heavily invested time or money in one of the big sharing sites—Flickr, Facebook, Picasa, or Photobucket—you'll be happy to know that a nice selection of apps is ready to help. (Alas, iPhoto fans, for now, you're out of luck; no Fire-friendly linking tool or app exists to grab your photos.) What follows, then, is a Fire-friendly tour of those four biggies:

- **FlickFolio for Flickr HD.** Costs a bit more ($3) than some of the freebie viewers available for other services, but it's a great tool if you're a hardcore Flickr user. With it you can browse all yours and your friends' photo collections; search by keyword, ratings, or tags; apply filters (show just those pix with three-stars or more, for example); add ratings and comments; play slideshows; and save to your Fire (tap, hold, and pick Save

Locally). You can do most of these things by tapping any photo (yours or others') once and, from the lower-right corner's downward-pointing triangle, picking from the list that appears: Info, Comments, Add to Favorites, View Photostream, Save Locally, and Send URL. Nice extra: Tap the search icon in the Options bar and enter any word or phrase (*cow, Terre Haute*) into the search box and get a collection on your Fire of public Flickr photos that match what you're looking for.

- **FriendCaster.** The way to go for Facebook picture browsing. Mucho-important beginners' tip: Rotate your Fire to landscape mode (sideways), or you won't see the Photos tab on the left side of the screen. From there, you can scroll through any of your Facebook albums or any that your friends have recently updated. You get nice, almost-full screen browsing. It's also easy to like, comment, and save favorites to your Fire. To do that, tap the upper-right, dog-eared photo icon. Pictures get placed in a Gallery album called FriendCaster. There's an ad-supported free version of this app; the $5 Pro model nixes those, plus lets you upload higher-res photos.

NOTE Facebook gets its own icon in the Fire's Apps Library, but that's a bit of a ruse. Tap it, and all you get is a shortcut to the social network's website (a mobile-friendly version, to boot). That said, the three horizontal stacked lines in the upper-left corner are worth checking out; tap that icon, and then tap the See My Albums link to browse your pix. Tap any of the thumbnail pictures in each of your albums, and from the page that appears, you can add comments or tap to download and save a pic to your Fire. FriendCaster, for now, is a better bet, mainly because it's easier to operate.

- **PicFolio for Picasa HD.** From the same developers as the FlickFolio app, this $1.50 utility does almost everything its sibling does, except it's for Picasa users. Browse albums, play slideshows, search, add comments and ratings. Plus, you can email photos and create new albums, neither of which you can do in FlickFolio.

- **Photobucket Mobile.** Very nice free app, and an easy way to tap into this popular online photo-sharing service. It features simple in-album browsing (swipe or tap the forward-arrow button), and you can upload pix if you like, share on Facebook or Twitter, or send via email. It's also a snap to download any pic to the Gallery app. Open the pic you want to save, then tap Options bar→Menu→Download. What you grabbed gets saved in Gallery→Pictures.

TIP In the Fire's web browser you can tap, hold, and save most images. Pick "Save image" from the pop-up menu and then find what you've picked in the Gallery app's Download collection. (This trick doesn't work on all sites. One lame omission: Google Images.)

Browsing the Gallery

You've gotten your photos and videos onto the Fire, organized them (or not), and, lo and behold, here comes Mrs. Kreplach from apartment 4H, always ready to show off *her* grandkids. Now's your chance to do a little photo bragging yourself. Launch the Gallery app (it's in the Apps Library), and the first thing you'll notice are one or more miniature photo piles. Each of these represent little photo and video collections. The number in parentheses following the pile's title indicates how many items are in the stack. Videos get a tiny Play button on the top image. Tap a pile, and you then see all that's inside: a neatly organized grid of however many photos or videos are in that folder.

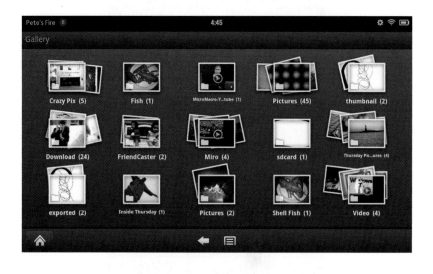

NOTE The icon at the screen's upper right represents the current layout view: either a nicely organized grid (two rows of three icons) or the currently pretty much useless date view. The latter, as explained back on page 108, chunks up a folder's contents into the dates and times when you imported the items onto your Fire—as opposed to the much more useful option of organizing according to when the photos were taken. Till that gets fixed, stick with grid view.

For humungo-sized folder collections—50 or more items—the Gallery offers an amusing effect. Hold your finger down and drag the grid either all the way to the left or right and the wall of images shifts, 3D-style, away from you. What's that good for? Impressing Mrs. Kreplach.

TIP One quick route back to the Gallery's highest perch—the grid of top-level photo stacks—is tapping the word *Gallery* in the upper-left corner.

Tap any picture to bring it front and center. Three buttons appear at the bottom of the screen for a few seconds after you tap. A slideshow icon lets you kick off a picture-after-picture show starting with the photo you just tapped (or any other in that folder). Zoom-out and zoom-in icons do what you'd expect (that is, the same thing you can do by pinching or spreading two fingers). Tap the photo once to bring those buttons back if they've gone away.

The menu button in the Options bar is your ticket to sharing and (limited) editing. (For sharing to work, you need to have an email app ready to transport your photos; Chapter 8 has the skinny on your options.) Tap the left-side Share icon and pick from any of the apps on your Fire that can dispatch a photo to other parts. (You won't see just email apps here; image editors and drawing apps show up too and are happy to accept photos for you to work on.) The middle button is for getting rid of pictures you no longer want on your Fire. Finally, the More button has a few choices worth a bit more explanation:

- **Details.** Tap for photo and video information, including things like the file name, its size, and the date (showing when the file was imported onto the Fire rather than when it was originally composed, as explained on page 108).

- **Crop.** This one's handy if you need to do a little pruning when you're out and about. Tap it, and an orange box surrounds the middle part of your photo. Hold and drag any of the sides to adjust the cropping area; what's inside the box is what remains. Tap Save when you're happy with the selected portion (or Cancel to abandon the idea). The Fire now gives you *two* files: the original, and the one you've cropped. (Movies don't get this option.)

- **Rotate Left/Right.** These two buttons do what they say. While you can achieve the same effect by rotating the Fire, these options *lock in* the rotational change.

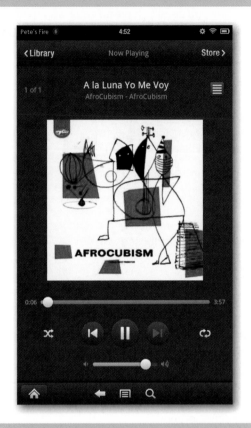

CHAPTER 7

Listening to Music

SHHHH, DON'T TELL APPLE (or its most loyal fanatics), but Amazon's built up one heckuva well-stocked, bargain-priced digital music service. Everything you buy comes with free online storage, which means never having to worry about backing up your purchases. And they've even designed a simple music-playing program that's less cluttered than iTunes and that can import most of the songs stored there. Take *that*, Cupertino.

The Fire, as you'd expect, takes full advantage of all this groundwork. And the device manages to overcome its relatively skimpy 8 GB storage capacity by tying its music player into the Amazon Cloud Drive (which, as page 31 explains, is where all your music gets stored). When you're in reach of a good WiFi connection, you barely notice—and don't even need to understand—the difference between songs streaming over the air and songs stored directly on your Fire. If you can make your way past the hours-long task of moving your music off your PC and up onto Amazon's online music locker, you'll be in tune heaven. This chapter shows you how to orchestrate everything: from finding and buying to organizing and listening.

Getting Music onto the Fire

Before hitting Play, you have to load up your virtual jukebox. You can pick from (and freely switch between) three different methods:

NOTE The Fire is happy to play a long list of different audio file types. This includes .mp3 and .m4a (the variety dispensed by iTunes). For a look at the complete alphabet soup collection, point your browser to *http://amzn.to/kfmm145*.

- **Transfer music from computer to Fire.** Got a well-stocked digital music collection already set up at home or in the office? Transferring files from one machine to the other—called *sideloading*—is simple. It's a quick way to load up an album or two. And if you haven't yet signed onto the idea of Amazon's everything-can-be-stored-in-the-Cloud philosophy, it's an easy way to quickly test out the Fire's music-playing abilities. Just plug the Fire into your PC or Mac and drag over the songs you want. Page 78 has a step-by-step guide.

- **Cloud Drive storage.** Long term, this route is the most convenient for most people. Upload your iTunes or Windows Media Player library to Amazon's web-based music locker and everything's ready to stream or download to your Fire. (Fringe benefit: You can play this cloud-stored music from *any* computer and most smartphones.)

  Two issues worth considering if you're thinking of going this route: time and money. If your music weighs in at multi-megabytes (anything north of, say, 20 albums), moving the load up to the Cloud Drive can take dozens of hours. It is, however, a one-time process, and Amazon's free utility program, the MP3 Uploader, offloads most of the work to computer gremlins while you work or sleep. The next section has the scoop. How much this'll cost varies. For most people, Amazon's $20 per year storage fee is sufficient; you can read a plain-English version of the fine print and notes on other plans starting on page 124.

- **Buying songs from Amazon.** Any music you buy from Amazon is ready to play more or less automatically on your Fire. Full coverage of your different buying options—on your Fire and on your regular computer—starts on page 135.

It's also possible to email a song or two to yourself. Given the size of these files—anywhere from 2 to 10 MB for a typical song—you wouldn't want to go crazy with this method. It's nice, though, in a pinch. Simply attach a song to an email message addressed to yourself. Use any email app on the Fire to open the message. (Chapter 8 is all about email.) From there, the exact steps vary based on which app you're using, but basically, you want to open or save the attachment in the Music folder. In the Fire's built-in email app, that's what happens automatically after you tap the Save button. You do, however, need to restart the Fire for the music to show up in your Music Library (the song appears in the Device section).

The Amazon MP3 Uploader

Amazon's no dummy. The company is aware that, over the past decade, most digital music fans use Apple's iTunes software and spend money in its companion store. Others use Windows Media Player, shop at places like eMusic, or just spend time *ripping* (that is, transferring) their CD collections onto their computers.

However you've gotten your music, chances are you store it on your computer and thus the challenge: how to get a collection that can easily weigh in it at 5 or 10 GB or more off your machine and onto Amazon's servers? Amazon's MP3 Uploader is the company's way of saying "Please, let us help." This one-trick pony includes a few extras that make it especially attractive. For example, if you've painstakingly created playlists, it can preserve them. If you don't have a continuous 83 hours to finish your upload, it does a nice job of stopping and then restarting where it left off (allowing you, for example, to start with your speedy work connection and finish off overnight at home). The tool also makes it simple to pick only those artists and songs you want to upload (why post duds you're never gonna listen to?).

Installing and launching the Uploader

The MP3 Uploader is free. Here's how to get it onto whichever computer has your music (you can install it on multiple machines if you've got tunes scattered about):

❶ **Start by visiting the Amazon Cloud Player (** *http://amzn.to/kfmm102* **).** This is a web-based music playing program, ready to play your tunes from any computer, smartphone, or tablet once you've moved them online. For now, however, this site is simply where you get to the Uploader. If it's your first time visiting the Cloud Player, you need to agree to some legalese before passing go.

❷ **In the upper-left corner, click "Upload your music."** Is the link, by any chance, dimmed out and not responding to your click attempts? Squashing this bug (which is what it is) is simple: Quit and restart your web browser. If that doesn't work, restart your computer. Once you've clicked the link, a small window launches; on it, click the "Download now" button.

❸ **Find the file that you've just downloaded.** In many cases it will show up right on your desktop. Or you may need to look in your Downloads folder (which goes by the same name on both Windows and Mac). The file you're looking for is called something like *AmazonMP3UploaderInstaller-1.0.7._ V164137419_.exe* (on a Mac it ends with the letters *dmg*).

❹ **Double-click and install the Uploader.** Inside the folder that opens, double-click *Install Amazon MP3 Uploader*. An Application Install window appears, including a note about a helper app called Adobe AIR. (This is software that Amazon uses to run the Uploader.) Change the installation location if you like (to do so, click the yellow folder icon) and then click Continue. Agree to yet another page of legal terms and—finally!—the Uploader launches.

The Uploader immediately starts looking for music on your computer, searching through either your iTunes or Windows Media Player collection. To cancel this hunt and pick the songs yourself, click "Stop and browse manually," and read on to the next section.

Choosing what to upload

The Uploader offers two routes to picking: the auto-sniffing option just described, or manually directing it to specific music-bearing folders. Option one is best if you use either iTunes or Windows Media Player to organize your music. Resort to option two only if you've purposely avoided those services and have your own music filing system.

If you've let the Uploader comb through your collection, you'll soon get a window summarizing, in a big beige bubble, what's currently on the upload ramp: all the playlists and individual songs stored in either iTunes or Windows Media Player. Included is the size of this bucket o' bits. Should this number exceed the 5 GB that Amazon gives you gratis, then you have to decide whether to pony up for additional space (page 124 covers your options) or pick a subset of songs from your collection that fits under the 5 GB limit. Use the expandable checklists to prune as necessary.

You'll also see a report estimating the time required. If your first reaction is "What the?...I have a job!" you're not the first. Fact is, all that music gathering over the past few years takes awhile to transfer from computer to cloud. Again, this figure isn't fixed; if you decide to pick and choose which files to upload, the time needed will shrink. Finally, when you're ready to make the transfer happen, give the "Start upload" button a click.

If you go in for the whole uploading enchilada, consider a few timesaving tips:

- **Use Ethernet rather than WiFi.** Connecting your computer to the Internet via a physical cable almost always boosts upload speeds. If you've been WiFi-only since the last Presidential administration, making the link isn't hard. You'll need, of course, an Ethernet cable (these are the ones whose plugs look like oversized telephone jacks). Insert it into your computer's similarly sized port and then again do the same on the back of your WiFi router. You should notice the transfer time required shrink down. In some cases you may need to restart your computer for the boost to kick in.

- **Find a faster Internet connection.** Your workplace bean counters may not be thrilled, but the fact is, most at-work Internet connections are speedier than those at home. The Uploader makes it easy to shift between both spots. Start, for example, at home, and when it's time to head off to the coal mines, click the Pause Upload button (which appears after you click "Start upload"). Once you're at work, click Resume to pick up where you left off. (The Uploader starts at the beginning of any partially uploaded file.)

- **Run the uploader overnight.** Let the transfer mules work while you sleep. Run through the steps outlined starting on page 121. When you're just about ready to pull the trigger, hold off until bedtime; then, press "Start upload" and let the files fly through the wee hours.

Buying More Storage

It happens in your home, it happens on your computer, and it may happen on your Cloud Drive: You've run out of room. Amazon's happy to rent you more space.

> **NOTE** If you buy music from Amazon's MP3 store, those purchases won't count against your storage limits. You do, however, need to tell Amazon to automatically stash those tunes in your Cloud Drive. Otherwise, Amazon downloads the music files directly (and only) to the device you're buying the tunes from. To do so, in the Cloud Player (page 131), go to Settings→"Your Amazon MP3 settings"; on the page that appears, click "Your MP3 purchases will be saved to Amazon Cloud Drive."

Plans run from $20 for 20 GB per year all the way up to a grand for 1,000 GB (known in tech talk as a terabyte). Beginning with the Fire's release, Amazon announced a "limited time" offer whereby most music files, purchased at Amazon or not, get stored for free. Sweet. (Eligible formats include MP3 and AAC files; look for the .mp3 and .m4a file extensions, respectively.) In most cases, if you're transferring music off a CD, you'll end up with MP3 files (which format exactly depends on the preference settings in your music-playing software); music purchased from the iTunes Store usually comes in the .m4a format.

To upgrade, log into your Cloud Drive and click the lower-left corner's "Buy additional storage" button.

From Cloud to Device: Downloading for Road Trippers

Transferring a song or album from the Music Library's Cloud section to the Device tab—for a long, WiFi-less car trip, say—is easy. Next to any Cloud-filed song or album is a white, downward-pointing arrow inside an orange square. You'll see it on pretty much every screen in this section, next to every playlist's name, as well as artist and allbum lists. To grab an individual song, tap and hold its title on any list. From the pop-up menu that appears, tap "Download song." Once you start a download you'll see a message appear briefly at the bottom of the screen "Song added to download queue" (or whatever you're downloading). Tap the Options bar Menu and

pick Downloads to see everything that's coming down (press the pause button to halt the proceedings) or the "See completed downloads" list below that to get a look at everything you've hauled down.

Should you wish to clear some songs off your Fire, you've got a few options. Tap and hold any song name and, from the pop-up menu, choose "Remove song from device." Serious spring cleaners may find it quicker to remove music in batches: by playlist, artist, or album. Tap and hold any of these items, and you get one of those "Remove...from device" choices in the pop-up menu that appears.

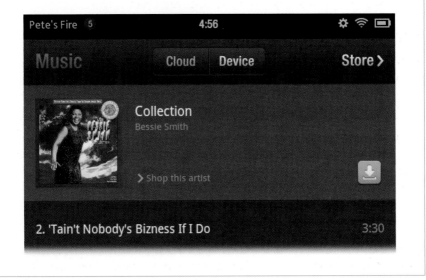

Browsing and Searching

Once your music is on the Fire (or within streaming range of it), head to the Music Library to start listening. Your first decision is whether to look behind tab #1 (Cloud) or tab #2 (Device). Tap either one to explore it, but keep in mind that these are separate collections. There's no way, in other words, to look at *all* the albums you own—you have to decide whether to look online or on device.

NOTE   Switching between Cloud and Device is simple enough, since those two tabs are visible on almost every screen in the Music Library. But wouldn't it be easier if Amazon subscribed to the Unified Theory of Music, in which all songs unite? Probably, but that's not how things work on the Fire, for now, anyway.

On the plus side, both areas are organized identically. Playlists, Artists, Albums, and Songs are the main browsing categories in both tabs. Each gets its own tour in the following sections.

Browse By Album, Artist, or Song

These three categories present similar-looking lists. About the only difference: The Artists list doesn't show album art on the left side, presumably because each artist can have more than one album. Scroll or flick to navigate from top to bottom in any list (for a refresher on both gestures, see page 25). As soon as you start moving downward, notice the gray tab that sprouts up on the screen's right side. Hold your finger on that little guy to move quickly, up or down, through large lists. A nice big letter, framed in white, appears center screen indicating where you'll stop. Handy.

Tap any artist's name, and the screen that appears lets you browse by song or album. Tap an album and you'll see a list of however many songs you've got. Most albums, of course, have about a dozen songs, but the only ones that show up on *your* screen are tracks you've stored on the Fire or up on the Cloud. When you see a song you like, tap it to play. (More details on various music-playing tips, tricks, and tactics in a moment.)

NOTE Playlists are custom song collections that you create—think of them as albums that you design. They're special enough to get extended coverage, which begins on page 133.

Search

As your collection grows, browsing to find a particular song can be a pain. Sometimes it's easier to get it Google-style. Tap the search monocle on the Options bar. Truth be told, this feature's not quite Google quality. What you can hunt for is pretty basic: artist, album, track, or playlist name. And you need to be in whichever silo—Cloud or Device—you wish to comb through. In other words: If you're in the Device section, the monocle won't pay attention to what's in the Cloud. There is, however, one way to get a birds-eye view of all your tunes. Tap out of the Music Library and head back to the home screen. Using the search oval up top, you can pull results from both Device and Cloud. (Not included: playlist names.)

Listening

Finally, the reason you came to this chapter in the first place: to play music. Whichever way you find the song you want—by searching, browsing, or playlist pecking—you hear tunage when you tap a song's title. That leads to a big snapshot of the album art front and center, surrounded by all the control buttons and status indicators you'd expect. From top to bottom, you get:

- **Track number/total tracks.** The first number indicates the slot this song occupies in its playlist or album. The second shows the total number of tracks in that collection.

- **Song title, artist, album.** Back when you were a hip youngster, understanding what was what was easy: *Gimme Shelter* was the song, *The Rolling Stones* were the band, and *Let It Bleed* was the album. Nowadays you might want to bookmark this page so you can help decipher which is which: *Chrome Posse*; *Jug Mine*; *Stuperific*. For the record: On top is the track name, below that comes the artist, followed by the album.

- **Now Playing button.** Ahead, the full skinny on this somewhat useful service. The short version: an insta-list of which songs lie in your immediate future.

- **Album art.** Looks great on the Fire's big screen, but it's not just for gawking. Tap and hold to get a useful pop-up menu with these choices: "Clear Now Playing Queue" (flush out everything in the Fire's "what to play next" short-term memory, including the currently playing song); "Download song" (you get this one if you're streaming something off the cloud); "Remove from Now Playing" (nix the current song from the list of that name); "View album/View artist" (a one-tap shortcut to a page listing the albums and songs in your collection of this artist); and "Shop artist in store" (Amazon's customized tour of everything it sells related to the song you're playing).

- **Progress bar.** Time lapsed appears on the left end, total time on the right. Press, hold, and move the white dot to hear a different part of the song; a time stamp pops up to indicate where, exactly, you're moving to.

- **Shuffle.** Tap these crisscrossing arrows to randomize the order of whatever collection you're currently in (playlist, album). The first tap turns the arrows orange and signals that the shuffle is on. Tap again to return to white; everything once again plays in order.

- **Previous/next track, pause/play button.** All of 'em work just as they have since the first cassette recorder. Not here: rewind and fast forward options. To do either, drag the Progress bar's white button.

- **Repeat.** Looks like two arrows chasing each others' tails. Tap once to loop, over and over, whatever group you're playing. (That is, once the last song finishes, the first one starts, and the cycle repeats.) Tap again and you'll see a tiny "1" inside a circle; that's the signal that the current song is set to play again and again and again.

- **Volume.** This slider works identically to the one in the Quick Settings menu. All the way to the left mutes the sound, the opposite end is as loud as it gets.

The "Now Playing" Queue

The Fire automatically creates this special "play these songs next" list for you. It's a handy way to keep the tunes flowing without having to do much work. Just tap a song title to play, and the Now Playing list fills up with that song *and* every song that follows in whatever list it's part of. If you don't care to hear all that, simply tap another song from somewhere else in your collection. Whatever list your just-tapped song comes from wipes out the current Now Playing list. You can also add individual songs to this list while browsing. Tap and hold any song's title and, from the pop-up menu, choose "Add song to Now Playing."

> **NOTE** Here's one place you're free to mix and match Cloud- and Device-stored songs.

You can check what's coming up on the Now Playing list in a couple of ways. One easy route: At the bottom of all list views, including those you see when shopping, tap the Menu button (on the Options bar; page 23) and then pick Now Playing. Another option: Tap the Now Playing icon on any song's album art screen (it's labeled back on page 128).

Unfortunately, you can't fine-tune the Now Playing list. You can't change the order in which the songs are played, for example. Instead, what you *can* do is remove individual songs from the list or clear out the whole list and rebuild it. To do the first, tap and hold any song's name and then pick "Remove from Now Playing." To flush the list, choose "Clear Now Playing Queue" from the same menu. To brew up some seriously customized song mixes, you need a playlist. That's covered in the next section.

> **TIP** Serious music fans like to fine-tune their tunes with an equalizer—a collection of bass, treble, and related settings that can be tweaked to make your songs sound better. The Fire has a decent collection of canned settings (Classical, Hip Hop, Rock, and so on). Turn it on by going to the Options bar→Settings and turning on "Enable equalizer modes." Right below that option is where you can pick the genre you most frequently play.

SkyTunes: The Amazon Cloud Player

If you store songs in Amazon's Cloud Drive, you can play this collection from any computer thanks to the Amazon Cloud Player (*http://amzn.to/kfmm143*)—a web-based jukebox. If you've ever used iTunes, Windows Media Player, or just about any other music-playing program, you'll have no trouble getting the hang of the Amazon version. Cloud Player's main attraction is ease-of-operation. It's lean and frill-free. What you get is what you need: playlist creation, basic browsing (by album, artist, genre), sharing (to Facebook and Twitter), and, of course, tune-playing.

That said, you may never *have* to use this thing. If the Fire and, say, the Amazon MP3 App on your smartphone are your sole virtual turntables, then feel free to skip this box. You can do everything you might want to do on those devices—make and edit playlists, listen to music. But given this puppy's cloud-friendly talents, you may appreciate a quick tour if you ever find yourself in a musical mood, say, at work. That way, you can play DJ wherever you are. Its three main offerings:

- **Playlist creation.** The left-hand Create New Playlist is where to start. See page 133 for the brochure pitch on how playlists work and why they're handy. Enter a name in the New Playlist pop-up window and then click

whatever you just created in the left-hand column. Sweet feature #1: In the Your Cloud Drive Music section (upper left), click Songs. From here, you can turn on the checkboxes next to as many songs as you like, and then drag the whole schmeer into the list you just created. To edit any playlist, click its name. As you move your mouse over its song titles (without clicking anything), notice the downward-pointing arrow next to each entry in the Artist column. Here's where you can delete a song from a playlist (it remains in your overall collection) or add it to a different playlist (pick "Add to Playlist" and then choose from the drop-down list). To reorder songs: Click, hold, and drag to any position you like. Any playlists you create here automatically appear in the Fire's Music Library—in the Cloud section, of course.

- **Song playing.** Simply click a title to play any track. To play all the songs in a playlist, click its name and then click the yellow "Play all" button on top of the list. To play just a few songs, turn on the checkboxes next to the tracks you want and then click the yellow Play button at the top of the list. Standard controls for previous/next track, play/pause, mute, shuffle, and repeat are in the lower-left corner.

–continued–

- **Collection pruning.** One thing you can only do in the Cloud Player: Get rid of songs. If the presence of some tune or album is bugging you, or you're trying to slim down to meet a pricing plan's storage limit (page 124), click the Songs list, turn on the checkboxes next to the offending titles, and then click Delete. You can do the same in any playlist (the button you want there is labeled Remove). A handy shortcut for selecting lots of songs: Turn on the checkbox on the top left of any list (next to title); that immediately turns on all the checkboxes below it. Remember: You're deleting these songs from Amazon's servers, so make sure you've got a copy somewhere else, if you want them.

Playlists: Be Your Own DJ

Half the fun of the digital music revolution is the ability to instantly download almost any song you want. The other half? Playlists. These custom-made song collections are great for matching any mood you're in or task you have to tackle. Name 'em whatever you like: *Hip Hop Hooray*; *Music for Onion Chopping*; *Xavier's Turning Two!* You—not some overly opinionated artist or album-stuffing music industry executive—get to decide what songs the playlist contains. The best part is you can make as many as you like. Each occupies practically no space on your Fire or the Cloud Drive, since they're just a list of virtual pointers to whichever songs you pick. That means you can put that favorite track of yours on ten different playlists and you still only have one copy of the song.

NOTE   Browsing through playlists works pretty much the same as exploring Artists, Albums, and Songs (covered back on page 126). On the Fire, tap the Playlists tab to see your collection of custom songlists; tap any playlist title to see what's on it. Two special entries that get added to everyone's Fire: Latest Purchases and Latest Additions. Both contain just what you'd expect.

To build a playlist right on your Fire, head to wherever you've got music (the Cloud or the Device tab in the Music Library), choose the Playlists tab, and then tap "Create new playlist." A box pops up for you to name the playlist. Then you get taken to a screen called "Add Songs to Playlist." Use the search oval to hunt for particular songs or browse through the list of everything that's stored on your Fire, or in the Cloud. Tap the plus (+) button on the right side to add whatever songs you like. Tap the upper-right Done button when you're finished.

NOTE Playlists can only be made from whichever collection you're in when you tap "Create new playlist." So if you start out in your Device collection, you don't get to add songs from the Cloud.

If you'd like to rename, remove, or quickly add songs to an existing playlist, just tap and hold the playlist's name; a pop-up window shows you your options. Any playlist you construct out of your Cloud-based tunes automatically gets added— you guessed it—to the Amazon Cloud Player. (One extra step that's sometimes necessary to get Cloud-based playlists to show up on your Fire: Tap Quick Settings and then the Sync button.)

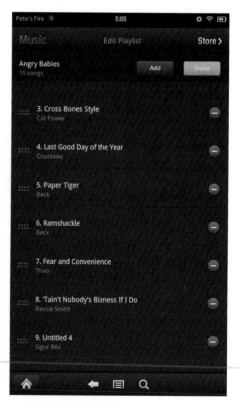

Editing an existing playlist is a snap. Navigate to one you want to change and then tap Edit in the upper right. An Add button appears, which you can use to search or browse through your collection. Tap the plus sign (+) next to any song you want to add; it gets pinned to the bottom of the existing playlist. To reorder the list, grab one of the left-side handles (two rows of four dots) and drag to whichever position you like. Use the right-side minus sign (-) to whack a title off the list. Tap the Done button when finished.

TIP   You can add albums or playlists to your home screen's Favorites shelves. Start by playing any song inside one of these; its album or playlist icon will show up on the home screen's Carousel (page 23). Tap and hold it there and pick "Add to Favorites." You can't add individual songs; if you pick their album art from the Carousel, you're adding the album or playlist to which it belongs. That said, you could construct a one-song playlist and add *that* to the Favorites list.

Browsing the Store and Buying

Amazon—surprise, surprise—makes it easy to shop for music. Whether browsing the regular web store (official name: Amazon MP3 Music Store) or Fire's built-in catalog, it's awfully tempting to spend lots of time...and money. You've been warned.

NOTE   Regardless of where you shop, you need to decide where to store the songs you buy. Option one: on Amazon's Cloud Drive, from which you can then stream or download tracks to your Fire or any computer. Option two: directly to whatever gadget you're shopping from—Fire or a regular computer. It almost always makes sense to stick things up on the Cloud Drive. Amazon doesn't charge extra to store music you buy from them. Plus, you'll always have a "master" copy up there and can then download or stream it to the Fire. Make your decision in the Music app by going to: Options bar→Menu icon→Settings→"Delivery preference." Make your choice on the pop-up list that appears.

On the Fire

The shortest distance between you and new music is the Music app's upper-right Store button. You'll see it on almost every music-playing screen. Tap it, and you get whisked off to a special Fire-only version of Amazon's music aisles. (Good news: You can keep playing songs from your own collection as you shop; at the bottom of the screen, there's a row showing your current track, along with previous, next, and play/pause buttons.)

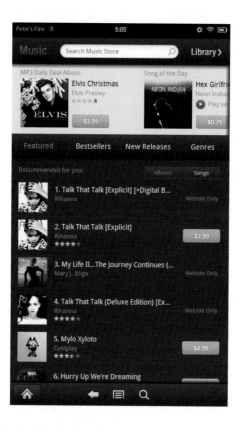

NOTE Got an Amazon gift card or promo code? Enter it on your Fire *before* you start shopping. Do so by going to Options bar→Settings→"Enter a claim code."

Once inside the store, you get a handful of different ways to search and browse. The theme here is simplicity. The inch-high top row (swipeable from left-to-right) posts a lineup of changing promo offers: the MP3 Daily Deal Album ($2 or $4 for up-and-coming artists), a Song of the Day (usually $0.69), a $5 MP3 Album, and so on.

The biggest chunk of the screen is occupied by "Recommended for you" selections. Choices here vary widely based on your recent purchases. It's all hip hop if you just bought Drake's latest; it's bluegrass if you recently got yourself some Alison Krauss.

Sandwiched between the top row and the recommended list are four links designed for browsing: Featured, Bestsellers, New Releases, and Genres. Tap any of the first three, and you get a list topped by tabs showing Albums or Songs. Head to the Genres section for deep dives. It's got about two dozen sub-categories (from Alternative Rock to Soundtracks), each of which gets broken down into further sub-sections. Hard Rock & Metal fans can celebrate the wonders of a world that includes everything from Death Metal to Live Albums. Christian & Gospel devotees get choices that include Christian Alternative, Christian Rap, and Praise and Worship.

Finally, there's a search oval on the top of the screen. A pretty underpowered search oval, that is. You enter a word or phrase (*rolling, let it*) and then get a finger-strainingly long list of results. At the bottom of really long lists, a Next Page button appears after the first 100 results. If you've got serious searching to do, read ahead to the next section for the web version of Amazon's MP3 Store.

Once viewing an album or song, check out a 30-second preview by tapping the play triangle to the left of the song title. To buy, or download a freebie, touch the orange button with either the price or the word FREE on it.

NOTE Some albums in the Fire's music shop feature an untappable Website Only message instead of the orange Buy button. Those contain digital extras that aren't, for whatever reason, Fire-friendly. Usually these are "digital booklets"—liner notes in PDF format. But wait! Didn't page 75 say that the Fire can display PDF files? And shouldn't you at least be able to view these booklets in the Documents app? Yes and yes. But, alas, you can't from within the Music app. Instead, head to Amazon's music shop on a regular computer, download the PDF-saddled album, and then transfer it over to the Fire using one of the methods explained starting on page 78.

Other services you won't find in the Fire's minimalist music store: reviews from fellow shoppers (or any way to add your own ratings); the ability to share song and album listings (via email, Facebook, Twitter); gift-giving or wishlist-adding buttons; and detailed information about the album (its length, the publishing label). For all this, and more, you need to head to the Web.

On the Web

No question: The Fire's music store makes shopping simple. But it's no match for the seriously fine-grained searching and playful categorization options you get in the full-fledged store. Oh, and another reason to visit the web shop: It's often got outrageously cheap (sometimes free, often heavily discounted) deals that you won't always, or easily, find on your Fire. Start by pointing your browser at Amazon's MP3 Music Store (*http://amzn.to/kfmm110*). Some of what you see here changes to match seasonal events. *25 Days of Free Holiday Music*, for example, helps get your jingle on for nothin'. Other web-only sections worth checking out are "Free Music from Rising Artists," "100 Albums for $5 Each," and "Free Songs & Special Deals." Links to all these are on the left-hand column of the Music Store's main page.

While it's *possible* to use the Fire's web browser to shop the MP3 Music Store, it's kind of a pain. The pages feel cramped on the Fire's small screen. If you do soldier on and buy a song or album there, the Store will suggest you switch over to the Fire's Music app to play it (as opposed to visiting the Amazon Cloud Player). Save your fingers and go ahead and do that. You'll get dumped back onto the Music app's Store section. To find your purchase, follow this trail: Library→Cloud→Playlists→Latest Purchases.

Your searching options on the big web store are plentiful. Type a word or phrase into the Search bar, and you can focus on any particular genre by picking from those listed on the left side of the page. So if you're looking for *tainted love*, you can choose to look at only the 11 country versions rather than all 680 results. You also get a handy grid of song titles, topped on the upper right by the super useful "Sort by" pop-up menu. Click that, and you can pick from listing options that include Popularity, Song Title (A to Z or vice versa), Price (High to Low, ditto), and Average Customer Review.

Tap any song's Play button to hear a 30-second sample. When you're ready to download a song, what you see after clicking either the Buy or the Get MP3 button (the latter's for freebies) depends on the choice you made earlier about where to store your music (page 124). If you opted to store everything in the Cloud, that's where your tunes automatically reside. Play what's there using your web browser to launch the Amazon Cloud Player (page 131). On your Fire, downloads await in the Music app's Cloud section.

If you want to download the music files to your computer, you need to install a freebie utility program called the MP3 Downloader. This software grabs any music you get on the MP3 Store and automatically stashes it in your iTunes, WMP collection, or wherever you like. See *http://amzn.to/kfmm125* for simple instructions on how to make this happen.

Other Tunes, Other Voices

What's in your Music Library isn't the only audio game in town. Audiobooks, for example, are a popular listening option; they get full coverage starting on page 50. But even when it comes to music, you gotta give Amazon credit: They've opened the Fire to all sorts of music app purveyors—many of which supply you with tools to shop somewhere *other* than Amazon. Below, a few of the more useful options you'll find in the Fire's App Store.

- **Pandora (free).** One of the oldest and most popular online music sites. It lets you pick artists you like and then builds a custom- ized radio station around your choice. As with regular radio, you can't specifically search for and play a song. But if you don't like what's currently on, you can tap the "next track" button (for a maximum of six taps an hour due to licensing restrictions). Pony up for a $36 per year subscription if you want to nix the visually annoying pop-up ads.

- **Rhapsody (free to download; subscription, starting at $10/month, required).** This app's great for those with a deep need to listen to a li'l bit of every- thing. Search through

or browse a catalog of 13 million songs. Create and even download playlists—perfect for away-from-WiFi trips. Here's something neat: When you search for an artist, the results list is topped by Play Artist Radio, a custom-station brewed up from bands or singers who resemble your chosen artist's music profile. There's also a lineup of Internet radio stations that's not overwhelming to browse. Like what you hear when listening? If the tune is in Rhapsody's catalog, you can tap to add it to your library or a specific playlist.

- **Stitcher (free).** A must for serious podcast fans, this is a huge, random sampling of high-profile shows, all for free—ESPN: The B.S. Report with Bill Simmons, This American Life, TEDTalks, Car Talk, This Week in Tech—the list is really long. It doesn't quite match every last item in iTunes, but most of the biggies are here,
plus you get a built-in list of terrestrial radio stations. Look up whatever station you like by state. Two weak areas worth noting: You can't download podcasts, and if you're a world music or radio fan, pickings here are slim.

—continued—

- **Slacker Radio (free; subscription gets you extras).** This app's best for people who have a specific genre in mind—60s rock, house, or classic jazz, for example—and don't want to spend much time browsing. Instead, simply dial up a hand-picked Internet radio station built around that preference. So if you're into alternative, you get a list of 14 choices (Indie Chill, 90s Alternative, Punk). Choose the one you want and if it's, say, 80s Alternative, you get a hand-picked mix of The Cure, Depeche Mode, New Order, and so on. No signup is necessary for basic service, but some of the best goodies are available only to paying subscribers. The Radio Plus service costs $4 per month and eliminates all ads, lets you skip any song you don't want to hear, and shows song lyrics. The $10 per month Premium Radio plan gets you all that plus any song on demand, single-artist stations, playlist creation, and caching (saving) albums and playlists for offline play.

- **TuneIn Radio (free; Pro version, $0.99).** A great way to turn your Fire into a radio replacement. Dial up all your local faves or browse some pretty ginormous categories dedicated to news, sports, and talk—each of which gets a slew of sub-categories. Also browse worldwide or according to language. Handy feature: Most stations offer an upper-right bullet-point icon when they're playing; tap it and then pick "See complete schedule" for a list of what's next. The Pro version lets you record stations and shows.

- **Scanner Radio (free; Pro version, $2.99).** If you've had enough music and news, why not spend some time listening to WKR- Cops? Scanner radio fans have made the Web a rich source of these streamed feeds. This simple app has newbie-friendly tools for finding action-packed stations (Top 50) as well as browsing and search tools for veterans of these sometimes riveting, often boring channels. Bonus treat: In the Options bar, the 10-Codes tab has a list of common police radio shorthand. It's not just the ones you know like 10-4, but some (hopefully) less common variants: 10-45, Animal carcass at...; 10-54, Livestock on highway; and 10-98 Prison/jail break. Archived call logs are available with a paid subscription to RadioReference.com, and an ad-free experience is yours if you spring for the Pro version.

Communications and Browsing

CHAPTER 8

Email and Address Book

NOWADAYS, EVEN AUNT IDA'S barebones phone can send and receive email. And if you're like the average, early-adopting Fire owner, you probably pack an Android or iPhone that works fine as a portable messaging machine. Just because Amazon included email on the Fire doesn't mean you have to use it. Why would you want to? Two reasons:

- **Bigger screen.** As much as thumb-calloused BlackBerry veterans love their speedy little keypads, even they'd admit their phone's mini screen makes tasks like attachment reading and message revision tough. The Fire's jumbo display (at least in comparison) makes plowing through a crowded inbox much more pleasurable. And the nearly adult-sized keyboard is souped up with some helpful typing aids (see page 25 for the full scoop).

- **Sharing.** The Fire may earn its bread as a personal media center, but we live in a social age, right? Everywhere you swipe—in the Gallery app, the Silk web browser, while shopping—you get a chance to send digital dispatches to email pals. Amazon's built-in email app ensures that, pretty much wherever you are, you can send off a quick note.

And, bless Amazon's world-conquering heart, they resisted the temptation to saddle you with yet another email account. The built-in app plays nice with big email providers like Gmail, Yahoo, and AOL. If you use a service that's not on the ready-to-use list, you can easily add it. (For example, some third-party apps cover Microsoft's Exchange email.) The companion Address Book is similarly friendly and ready to do helpful things like import your existing contacts. Read on to find out how to get it all connected.

NOTE With email and contacts accounted for, where's the third Musketeer? Page 224 covers a few options for turning the Fire into a digital calendar.

Email and Address Book Setup

Like any email program, the one that comes on every Fire—called Email, as it happens—needs info from you to perform its postal duties. Setup is a snap for your Google, Yahoo, Microsoft (Hotmail), or AOL account. Follow these steps:

❶ **In the Fire's Apps Library, find and then tap the Email icon.** You'll find Email already installed in the Device section of Apps.

❷ **Tap Start, and then choose your email provider.** A screen appears listing the four ready-to-go email providers. If you use one of these services, tap its name. If someone else handles your email, tap Other. You'll have to round up a bit more information about your account. Amazon's put together a handy chart (*http://amzn.to/kfmm129*) listing most of the info you need to gather. See page 150 to find out the remaining hoops you need to jump through.

Pete's Fire ③	9:51	⚙ 📶 🔋

Select E-Mail Provider

Select an e-mail provider from the list below

Gmail

Yahoo

Hotmail

Aol

Other

NOTE There's one group of people who won't get much out of the Email app: Microsoft Exchange users. This system is most often found among mid-sized and large corporations. If that includes you, you'll need help from a third-party app like Enhanced Email or Exchange By Touchdown (both of which, incidentally, also keep your calendar and contacts in sync).

❸ **Enter the user name (that is, your full email address) and password for the email account you chose in Step 1.** Need a Keyboard 101 refresher? Page 25 has the basics. If you're still getting the hang of Fire typing, turn on the Show Password checkbox; that way you can make sure you've entered it correctly. When you're done here, tap Next.

❹ **Type the name you want to appear on the email messages you send.** Ever wonder why some people's email identifies them as *Kardashian Kim* or *WINFREY O*? They (or their now unemployed assistants) messed up this simple but often overlooked step. What you need to do is enter your first name followed by your last name: *Yogi Bear*. Now everyone who receives your email will see your name correctly displayed. The optional Account Name box is useful if you use more than one email service. The name you enter here helps you tell which account you're checking.

❺ Select your other options. You have a couple more choices to make on this screen. You may want to turn on the "Send mail from this account by default" checkbox if this is your main email service. That way, any other app that uses Email's services (the web browser, when you forward links; the Gallery app, when you send off pictures) will automatically compose messages from this account. You can always change to another account, on a case-by-case basis.

The "Import contacts" checkbox is a nice way to auto-fill the Contacts app, which you'll meet later in this chapter (page 169). Turn this on, and the app gets access to the list of names, email addresses, and phone numbers you've probably already stockpiled in your chosen email. If you'd rather start fresh, leave this box unchecked.

NOTE Unfortunately, not all members of the address book family make the trip from Web to Fire. You get every contact's email address(es) and phone number(s), but none of the extra info, like snail mail addresses, birthdays, and special notes. You can get two of these additional items onto the Fire—postal address and company/title info—but you need to manually import your contact list. Page 158 explains how.

❻ Finish up by tapping "View your inbox." After a few seconds of email fetching, Email presents you with a list of the 25 most recent messages you've received. Tap any message to read what it says. (A full explanation of how to check and send email starts on page 159.)

To add another email account, head to the Accounts page (Options bar→Menu icon→Accounts). Tap that page's Menu icon and choose "Add account." Go back to Step 2 and repeat the cycle for each additional account.

Manually Adding Account Information

If your email provider isn't on Email's quick setup list, you'll need to track down and enter a few details yourself. Tap Other, as described in Step 2 on page 148, and then do the following:

❶ Enter your login details. Type the exact user name and password you use to access your email. Tap Next when you're done.

TIP If you've already got an email account up and running, you can also get to this screen by heading to the Accounts screen in Email, tapping the Menu button on the Options bar, and then picking "Add account."

❷ **If necessary, pick your account type: POP3 or IMAP.** In some cases, the Email app knows which of these transmission standards your email provider uses. If that's the case you won't have any decision to make here and can skip to the next step. If you are seeing a screen asking *What type of account is this?* the simplest route to an answer is checking the Help section on your email provider's website. The difference between the two account types is interesting mainly to email historians. IMAP has won this standards battle and provides one key convenience not available to POP3 users: It coordinates everything you send and receive across all the various smartphones, tablets, and computers you use to do email. Send or delete a message from one gadget, and that change gets mirrored instantly across all your gadgets. With POP3, you have much more work to do. You must manually coordinate your email across multiple devices. (A decade or so ago this wasn't a problem, when most people used only one computer to check email.) Tap Next.

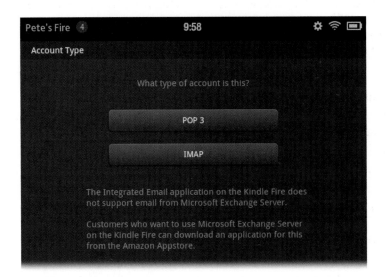

❸ **Fill in the "Incoming server settings" boxes.** The boxes and pull-down menus on this screen all work together to pull down any mail sent your way. In many cases, the Email app will try to automatically enter all the correct settings info here. In practice, this is a mixed blessing. If, after tapping Next, you get a message saying "Setup could not finish," then tap "Edit details." At that point you have a few options. First, consult Amazon's Help page (*http://amzn.to/kfmm129*) for a chart listing common settings. If you can't find the magic numbers you need there, your best bet is to call your email provider or visit its Help page. Even with the most lucid explanation ever written of these options, without the specific settings chosen by your company, you'll never figure out what to enter.

Incoming server settings

Username

peter.meyers@mindspring.com

Password

••••••••

POP3 server

pop.mindspring.com

Security type

None

Authentication type

PLAIN

Port

110

Next   Cancel

Manual Settings for Some POP3/IMAP E-mail Providers

POP3/IMAP Account	Server Type	Incoming Server	Security Type	Authentication Type	Incoming Port	Outgoing Server	Security Type	Authentication Type	Outgoing Port
Aim.com	IMAP4	imap.aim.com	None	Plain	143	smtp.aim.com	SSL (Always)	Automatic	465
aol.com	IMAP4	imap.aol.com	SSL (Always)	Plain	993	smtp.aol.com	SSL (Always)	Automatic	465
att.net	IMAP	imap.mail.yahoo.com	SSL (If Available)	Plain	993	smtp.mail.yahoo.com	SSL (If Available)	Automatic	465
bellsouth.net	IMAP	imap.mail.yahoo.com	SSL (If Available)	Plain	993	smtp.mail.yahoo.com	SSL (If Available)	Automatic	465
charter.net	IMAP4	mobile.charter.net	SSL (Always)	Plain	993	mobile.charter.net	SSL (Always)	Automatic	587
comcast.net	POP3	mail.comcast.net	SSL (Always)	Plain	995	smtp.comcast.net	SSL (Always)	Automatic	465
earthlink.net	POP3	pop.earthlink.net	None	Plain	110	smtpauth.earthlink.net	None	Automatic	587
gmail	IMAP4	imap.gmail.com	SSL (Always)	Plain	993	smtp.gmail.com	SSL (Always)	Automatic	465
hotmail	POP3	pop3.live.com	SSL (Always)	Plain	995	smtp.live.com	TLS (always)	Automatic	587
icloud.com (mobile me)	IMAP4	imap.mail.me.com	SSL (Always)	Plain	993	smtp.me.com	None	Automatic	587
Inbox	POP3	my.inbox.com	None	Plain	110	my.inbox.com	None	Automatic	587
live.com	POP3	Pop3.live.com	SSL(Always)	Plain	995	smtp.live.com	TLS(Always)	Automatic	25
Mail	POP3	pop1.mail.com	SSL(Always)	Plain	995	smtp1.mail.com	None	Automatic	587
me	IMAP4	imap.mail.me.com	SSL (Always)	Plain	993	smtp.me.com	None	Automatic	587
msn.com	POP3	pop3.live.com	SSL (Always)	Plain	110	smtp.live.com	TLS (Always)	Automatic	587
pacbell.net	IMAP4	imap.mail.yahoo.com	SSL (If Available)	Plain	993	smtp.att.yahoo.com	SSL (If Available)	Automatic	465
sbcglobal.net	IMAP4	imap.mail.yahoo.com	SSL (If Available)	Plain	993	smtp.att.yahoo.com	SSL (If Available)	Automatic	465
snet.net	IMAP4	imap.mail.yahoo.com	SSL (If Available)	Plain	993	smtp.att.yahoo.com	SSL (If Available)	Automatic	465
swbell.net	IMAP4	imap.mail.yahoo.com	SSL (If Available)	Plain	993	smtp.att.yahoo.com	SSL (If Available)	Automatic	465
verizon.net	POP3	incoming.verizon.net	None	Plain	110	outgoing.verizon.net	None	Automatic	587
yahoo.com	IMAP4	imap.mail.yahoo.com	TLS (If Available)	Plain	143	smtp.mobile.mail.yahoo.com	SSL (If Available)	Automatic	465

Once you've filled everything in, tap Next.

➍ **Fill in the "Outgoing server settings" boxes.** Same deal as in the previous step, except this screen is for the messages you send.

➎ **Decide how often you want Email to check this account.** From the "Folder poll frequency" list, pick the setting you want: Every 15 minutes, 30 minutes, hourly, or manually. The first three check at those regular intervals; the last one means that Email fetches new email only when you tap the "Check mail" button (two arrows chasing each others' tails) on the Options bar.

➏ **Pick the name you want to appear on the emails you send.** Your work from here on out is identical to those using the quick setup email providers. Head back to Step 4 on page 149 and follow those instructions to the finish line.

NOTE To get rid of an account, navigate to the Accounts page, tap and hold the name of whichever one you want to delete, and then pick "Remove account" from the pop-up list.

Fine-Tuning Email's Settings Options

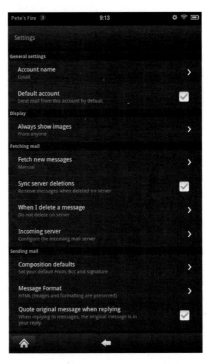

The Email app's standard settings are what most people will want, most of the time. Occasionally, though, some fiddling is called for. Perhaps you want to change how often the app fetches your messages, add a chime to signal new arrivals, or customize your note-ending signature? For all this, and more, open either the Email's Unified Inbox (page 159) or any individual email account you have, and then head to Settings (Options bar→Menu button), and then read on.

- **General settings.** *Account name* is the for-your-info-only header that appears on Email's Accounts page. Tap to revise the one you initially created. *Default account* is meaningful everywhere else on the Fire, outside of the Email. It's how you choose which email account gets used to, for example, to share photos, web page links, and so on. Stick a checkmark in this box to dub this account the chosen one.

- **Display.** This one-setting section—*Always show images*—gives you a nice way to cut down on visual clutter in your email. You get three choices to pick from in this pop-up menu: "No," "From contacts," and "From anyone." The first option means no images ever appear in your email messages. Instead, you get a Show Pictures button at the top of any picture-bearing message. Tap it to make images appear wherever its author intended (if you don't tap, the image's onscreen space is left blank). "From contacts" auto-loads images only from people in your address book.

- **Fetching mail.** This batch of options controls all the messages you receive. *Fetch new messages*: Pick between Manual (you tap the "Check mail" button on the Options bar to pull down new messages) and Push (Email automatically grabs messages as they arrive on your email provider's server). *Sync server deletions*: A checkmark here means that every message you trash on your email provider's master server also gets cut here. So if you're doing email in a web browser and you clear out a bunch of messages, they'll also get wiped on your Fire. When this checkbox is empty, no such synching happens. *When I delete a message*: Same as the previous setting, except here it works in the *other* direction. That is, if you choose, from the pop-up menu, "Do not delete on server," any message you trash on your Fire remains on your email provider's master machine. The next two choices—"Delete from server" and "Mark as read on server"—do what they say. *Incoming server*: A way back into the sending-settings minutiae that you read about in Step 3 on page 151.

- **Sending mail.** *Composition defaults*: Make your messages look just so with the choices here. Pick the name your emails appear sent from using the "Your name" box. "Your email address" works only for some email providers (Gmail being a notable exception): In it you can "spoof" your sending address, entering any email address you like. A favorite trick among spammers, most law-abiding netizens frown on this kind of identity cloaking. "Bcc all messages to" is often used by task management geeks: Sending a copy of every message you fire off to yourself is one way of keeping tabs on everything you ask other people to do. Turn on the Use Signature box and fill in its affiliated field if you want to tag all your outgoing emails with your contact info, favorite quote, or other boilerplate poetry. Here's also where you can kill that adver-signature from Amazon ("Sent from my Kindle Fire"). Finally, the "Signature position" radio button indicates where to append any signature you create: "Before quoted text" or "After quoted text" (relevant, of course, only when you're replying to a message).

Message format: Choices here are Plain Text or HTML. The first ensures that anyone, no matter how his email program is configured or what its capacity (some choke on or flat out reject images), sees exactly what you send him. The limitation, as the name suggests, is that you can only send simple text messages, with no fancy formatting or embedded pictures (you can, however, always attach images or any other kind of file to a plain-text message). Pick HTML, and you can fancy up your messages with as much formatting as your email sending program offers. Since there are no formatting tools in the Email app's message composer, this option only matters if you're pasting in formatted content copied from somewhere else (a web page, for example).

Quote original message when replying: A simple yes/no decision to make by either turning on or off this checkbox. Including the full text of the original message in a response is helpful for recipients who, a week after emailing you are trying to figure out what you mean by "Great! Let's go with option 2."

Outgoing server: Your path back to the sending settings you specified in Step 4 on page 153.

- **Folders.** The five folders listed here (Archive, Drafts, Sent, Spam, Trash) can each be synched with any folder you like on your email provider's "master" (that is, online) server. Most people can safely bypass doing any-thing here. But if you do, for some reason, want to funnel your Fire email into special folders on your web-based email account, you'd make that happen here. For example, say you wanted to keep track of messages sent from your Fire. First step in this scenario is to create a folder named "Sent from Kindle Fire" up on the web-based version of your email account. Then, back on the Fire, navigate to this area in Settings, tap the Sent folder, and tap again the "Sent from Kindle Fire" listing that appears in the pop-up box. (Give the Fire a few minutes to recognize any folders you create online.)

- **Notifications.** Time to have some fun here, if you're easily amused by beeps, chimes, and their silicon successors. Pick from a list of about 20 options (Caffeinated Rattlesnake, Moonbeam) to let you know when new mail arrives. If none of this sounds appealing, go for Silent.

Pete's Fire 3	9:14	⚙ 🛜 🔋

Notification Sound

Silent ●

Caffeinated Rattlesnake ○

Captain's Log ○

Dear Deer ○

Don't Panic ○

Heaven ○

Highwire ○

Kzurb Sonar ○

Look At Me ○

Missed It ○

Moonbeam ○

| OK | Cancel |

Filling Up the Contacts App

Earlier in this chapter you learned how to quickly download an online contacts collection (page 150). But what if you don't store your Rolodex on the Web? Maybe you keep it in one of those old-fashioned computer-based programs like Outlook or the Mac's Address Book. Getting that info onto your Fire is crucial. Tapping out addresses, character by character, each time you send an email can get old, quickly. The Fire offers two options, both of which start by launching the Contacts app (find it in the Device section of the Apps Library).

Another reason to pursue one of the following manual methods: The Email app's auto-import feature doesn't grab your pals' snail mail addresses. If you'd like that info, these procedures make that possible.

- **Method one: Manually add individual contacts.** No, you wouldn't want to fill your entire address book this way. But it's fine for punching in the details of your seatmate on a long flight. Hit the Menu button on the Options bar and pick "New contact." The boxes that appear in the Name section are self-explanatory: Tap each one ("Name prefix," "First name," and so on), enter what you like, and then hit Save Changes. The labels in both the Phone and Email sections (both of which initially appear saying Home) are tappable; do so to pick from a long list of options, clearly written by someone with a long history in telecommunications (Telex? ISDN?). One useful choice at the end of the Email label list: Custom. Tap it to create a category for pals with more than just work and home email addresses. To add multiple phone or email entries, tap the plus (+) button on the right side of the screen, across from the section name.

The plus (+) buttons next to "Postal address" and "Organization" launch, respectively, boxes with all the usual snail mailing particulars (street, PO box) and ones for Company and Title. Finally, add a picture to any contact by tapping the upper-right corner's image icon. The Fire switches you over to the Gallery app (page 114). Navigate to the picture you want, use the cropping arrows if you like (page 117), and then tap Save. When you're finished entering all the info you want, tap Save Changes at the bottom of the "New contact" screen.

- **Method two: Import a contact list.** Have an address book stored on your regular computer? This one's for you. The only format the Fire accepts is the industry standard vCard, so step one is to export your contacts into a vCard file. You can take all of your contacts or only some of them.

  Once you've got a vCard file loaded up, the next step is getting it onto the Fire. Use either of the methods described starting back on page 77: Transferring via USB connection or beaming over a WiFi connection. (Sorry, you can't email the vCard file.) You want to stash the file in your Fire's Download folder. That's where the Contacts app looks when you commence importing. To make that happen, in Contacts, tap the Menu icon on the Options bar and then choose Import/Export. On the pop-up list, tap "Import from internal storage." Ingestion time depends on the size of your contacts list. Count on about five minutes for every 1,000 contacts.

> **NOTE** Some pesky downsides in this whole process remain unaddressed at the time of this writing. Biggest is synching. What happens if you change or add a new contact on your main address book (be it web- or computer-based)? The Fire has no way of incorporating those changes. Your options range from lame to inconvenient. First, you could manually enter any changes on the Fire that you make on your main list. Ugh. Or, you could wait till you make a few changes, delete the Contacts app's contents (as described in the next note, and then re-import the fresh load. That's still not ideal. Best hope, long term, is for Amazon to beef up its Contacts powers, or wait for a third-party app to address this issue.

There's not much to actually using the Contacts app. It's a big list that you can scroll or search through. For a tour of its main talents, see page 169.

> **NOTE** To empty out everything stored in Contacts, go to Quick Settings→More→Applications, choose All Applications from the "Filter by" menu, and then scroll down to and tap Contacts Storage (not the one before it: Contacts). In the Storage section, tap Clear Data and—woosh—everything's gone.

Checking and Reading Email

Once you've got your message machine humming, it's time to see what the inbox holds. Launch the Email app by going to the Device section of the Apps Library. (Want to make it a home screen favorite for faster access? Page 24 explains how.) Most of the time you'll arrive on the Accounts page—a simple list of every email account you've set up. Even if you make do with just one email address, you'll still see this page, which starts with a Unified Inbox. Tapping this option shows you an aggregate tally of all your email, regardless of which address it was sent to. Below that are listed one or more individual email accounts, each containing all the messages sent to that address. Dive in wherever you like: Unified Inbox or an individual account inbox.

Opening any inbox automatically triggers a go-fetch command—at the top of the screen you see a "Checking mail" mini-banner. If the app finds something, the new stuff appears at the top of the inbox, and a white info box at the bottom of the screen lets you know how many emails arrived. This page lists the 25 most recent messages; to pull down more, scroll to the bottom of the list and tap "Load up to 25 more."

NOTE The next time the Email app checks depends on the schedule you set back on page 153. Or you can check anytime you like by tapping the "Check mail" button (two arrows chasing each others' tails) in the Options bar.

Tap to open any message. If it's too long to fit on the screen, scroll down to read to the end. If it's too wide, swipe right to left to view the outer edges, or rotate the Fire and see if the 90-degree shift fits everything onscreen. To see who else, if anyone, got this note (either as a top-tier To recipient or as a Cc spectator), tap the downward-pointing exposure triangle on the right end of the subject line.

Truncated subject line —

Complete subject line

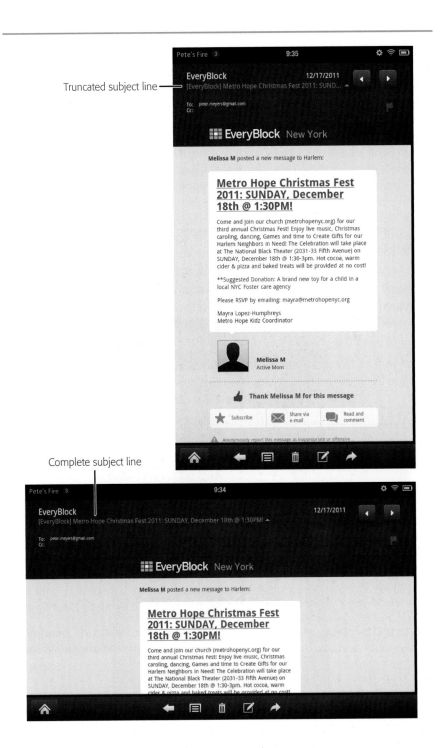

TIP   Can't see the full text of the subject line? Switch the Fire from vertical to horizontal, and that should give you enough room to get rid of the ellipsis.

A couple of options await for plowing through a big batch of newly arrived notes. If you've got a message open, the two arrows pointing left and right (upper-right corner) put you one tap away from the next message. Left arrow gets you up the list (to the newest arrivals); right arrow brings you further down toward the older emails. To look at your inbox from on high, tap the Back button in the Options bar. Back in this list view, you see a stack of messages, each with enough info showing to reveal who sent it, when it was sent, the subject line, and the first sentence or so.

The Email app gives you a few ways to organize what you see in this list, or weed out messages that aren't worth your time. In the upper-right corner's Organize By button, choose from one of eight different options: Newest, Oldest, Subject, Sender, Flagged, Read, Unread, Attachments. Pick one, and the inbox list reshuffles to reflect this new order.

The Edit List button is a good tool for some quick pruning. Tap it (Options bar→Menu button) and you can touch to select one or more messages in the list. As you do, the formerly dimmed-out buttons at the bottom of the screen light up, ready for action: "Mark as Read" toggles the message's summary header from bright white (a newly arrived, unread message) to dull gray (a message you've read, or at least glimpsed at). The magic of the "Mark as Read" button is that you don't even have to glimpse the email's contents. Use it to flick off messages that don't really need your attention—like the specials flyer from your local gerbil shop. On the other hand, if you've already read a message but want its bright white font to remain—reminding you that this note still merits attention worthy of a new message—then turn it from gray to white by tapping the "Mark as *Un*read" button.

The next button over is Move. This one lets you transfer one or more selected emails into any of your email account's subfolders. (These are folders you've previously created prior to your life with the Fire. Some people create enormously elaborate subfolder systems—Art, Art-History, Art-Friends—others never go beyond the usual assortment that most email providers create—Drafts, Inbox, Sent, Trash.) Delete and Done are the last two options: The first trashes any selected emails; the second is how you return to the main list.

TIP In list view, you can tap any dimmed flag icon (right side of the screen) to signal its importance (to you; the sender doesn't know you've flagged anything). You can do the same in any individual, open message, but in list view you can really blow through a big batch, flagging messages worthy of attention later on.

To track down a specific message, use the Email app's search tool. Either tap the search monocle in the Options bar or pull down any list to reveal the search oval. Searching works just as it does everywhere else on the Fire: Tap the oval to bring up the keyboard. Type to enter your word or phrase and then hit the virtual keyboard's Search button to unleash the hounds. Be aware, though, that your search is limited to the folder you're currently in—and covers only those messages loaded on your Fire (that is, not any hidden behind the "Load up to 25 more" link, as described on page 160). So if you're looking for that message you trashed three weeks ago, it's better to either do it on a regular computer where you can search through your entire email archive, or navigate to your email account's Trash folder and search through that.

NOTE To get to Trash, or any other folder mentioned in this section, tap the Folders button (Options bar→Menu button). Folders located directly on your Fire appear without any brackets around their name: Outbox, Inbox, Sent. You don't have a hand in making these: Each account creates them as necessary, whipping up a Sent folder, for example, the first time you send a message. Any folders with brackets around their name ([Gmail]/All Mail; [Gmail]/Drafts) are lodged up on the Internet server of your email provider; here's where, typically, you can build however many folders you like.

See a web link you want to visit? Tap it, once, quickly. The link turns orange, and the Fire's web browser whisks you off to where it's pointing. To copy, rather than visit, the web address, hold your finger on the link; a pair of selection tabs grab either end of the link. Tap either of these to copy it to the clipboard. Now use any text-writing app—Email itself or one of the word processing apps mentioned in Chapter 4—to paste it. Just wait for the cursor to appear, tap and hold a point on the screen, and then pick Paste from the pop-up list. You can also paste the copied web address into the address bar of the Fire's web browser, as explained on page 165. Incidentally, copying any ol' text in an email works the same way: Tap and hold any word you like. If you want to copy more than one word, first tap any word in the phrase you want. Once the selection handles appear, tap/hold/move either one to extend the selection band.

NOTE You can't copy an image from your email—at least not on the Fire. If there's an embedded figure you really want to hang onto, forward it to your computer's regular email program and grab it from there.

The Email app tries to guard against overstuffed emails clogging the Fire's limited storage. If a message is greater than 32 kilobytes, you see a black "Download complete message" bar at the bottom of the note. Tap to retrieve the remaining portion. Some messages arrive bearing cargo (a paper clip icon next to the sender's name is your clue). To open an attachment, scroll to the bottom of the page and tap Open (to view the image or document directly in the email) or Save (to stash it in the Download folder). To see what's inside this folder, use the Gallery app (for images; page 114) or a third-party file-viewing app, like Quickoffice (page 81) or WiFi File Explorer Pro (page 105).

When you're ready to reply, you face the same to-do list as when you compose a message from scratch. Read on to the next section for everything you need to know about that. To get your reply started, tap the rightward-curving arrow at the bottom of any open message and pick Reply (to respond to just the sender) or "Reply all" to include everyone (those in the To box as well as those in the Cc field). That same row is also where you find the Forward button; tap it and add one or more email addresses (page 166). And you don't even need to open an email to start the note-slinging process; in list view, just tap and hold any email snippet and a pop-up list gives you choices to Delete, Forward, "Reply all," Reply, "Mark as spam" (dispatches it to your spam folder), and "More from this sender" (downloads other messages from your online inbox).

Composing a Message

Ready to write? Head into the list view (page 159) of the account you want to send your email from—no choice to make here, of course, if you've only got one email address. Grab a blank page and virtual pen by tapping the "new message" icon (a pencil lying diagonally across a white box). Then:

❶ **Decide who's going to receive it.** Start in the To box. Either use the virtual keyboard to enter someone's address or tap the plus (+) button to pick from your Contacts list. To choose an address book entry, scroll down the list, or tap one of the right-hand margin's letters to skip to that point in the alphabet and then tap to pick the name you want. To add multiple recipients, repeat the process: Tap the plus button and pick another name. Timesaving tip: Start typing a contact's first or last name, and a list of matches drops down from the To box. Tap to select the one you want.

Message text

Sent from my Kindle Fire

NOTE To remove a name that you've added, tap the cursor and hit the backspace key until it's gone.

You probably know the drill regarding that Cc/Bcc button. Tap it for boxes bearing the same name—both work the same as the To field. The first is for recipients you want to include, and keep informed, but don't necessarily expect a reply from; the second is a sneaky, but totally legitimate way of sending someone a message without letting any of the To or Cc recipients know that someone else is also getting the same email. One especially good reason to use this cloak: when sending a message to a huge list (baby announcement, change of address). Many Internetians consider it bad form to publicly expose so many email addresses. After all, everybody already gets enough spam; why hang everyone's address out like that for cherrypicking? The solution lies in the Bcc box. Address the email to yourself and hide all the recipients' addresses in the secret box.

❷ **Fill out the Subject line.** There's no law saying you *have* to include a sub-ject. But, again, a best practice ritual has emerged. Recipients who face the Problem of Too Much Email find short, descriptive blurbs here helpful for wading through their daily message load.

❸ **Compose your message.** Tap the big box that says "Message text." An orange ribbon hangs off the cursor; that'll come in handy later if you need to edit what you've written. For now, it disappears after a few seconds, since there's no text to traverse. Type just as you would on a normal keyboard. Turn the Fire to landscape mode if you want bigger keys. (The tradeoff? A smaller writing window.) For a refresher on keyboard basics, turn back to page 25.

NOTE Resent being enlisted as Amazon's advertising agent and want to stop declaring that this email was "Sent from my Kindle Fire"? You can either manually delete it by tapping immediately to the right of the word "Fire" and hitting the backspace key till the thing's gone. Or remove it permanently by following the instructions on page 154. (That's also where you can insert a new signature of your choosing.)

❹ **Change, if you want, the account you're sending** *from*. This applies only if you've set up multiple email accounts (for work, home, and so on). A "Send as" pull-down menu appears below the message. If you want to switch to a different account, pick it here.

❺ **Add any attachments.** Another optional task: If you've got a document or image you want to send along with your message, tap the Attach but-ton. The choices that appear in the pop-up "Choose attachment from" list vary based on which file-managing apps you have installed on your Fire. At a minimum, you'll see Gallery (for pix) and Quickoffice (for Office files). Choose the one you want and then navigate to and tap to select the file you want.

❻ **Send your message.** If you want time to polish (or reconsider), tap Save Draft. When you're ready to get back to it, in list view (page 159), tap the Folders icon (Options bar→Menu button) and select the Drafts folder. Otherwise, tapping Send dispatches your note off into the ether. Cancel, of course, is for bailing out entirely.

The Contacts App

One upside to the built-in Contacts app's simplicity: Searching through it and other operational maneuvers is a breeze. Once you've filled it up, the thing looks like any other long list on the Fire. Swipe up or down to traverse the entries; tap any letter on the right to quickly jump to that spot in the alphabet. Tap the monocle on the Options bar to search. The app compares what you type to the letters that start the first *and* last names in your contacts list. For example, if Herman Melville is in your list, he'll appear on the auto-suggest list (page 90) once you enter *Her*, *Herm*, *Mel*, *Melvi*, and so on. But if you tap in *ville*, you get no results.

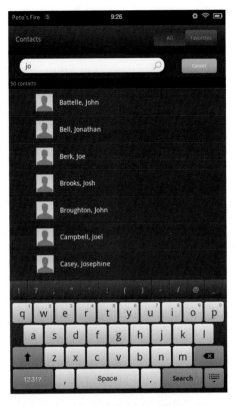

If your little black book is especially thick, consider making it easier to find frequent correspondents by tagging them as "favorites." Do so either when you've tapped open an entry (tap the dim star in the upper-right corner). Or, when you're on the main list screen, tap, hold, and choose "Add to favorites." Then, whenever you like, select the Favorites tab to see just your chosen few. That pop-up menu is also where you can do things like edit, delete, and whip up a quick email to the chosen contact.

You'll find two choices in the Settings menu (Options bar→Menu button): First is "Sort list by." You can sort by either first or last name. Whichever you select determines the alphabetization order on the Contacts main list. "View contact names as" offers similar options: "First name first" (George Washington) or "Last name first" (Washington, George).

TIP   Want to see a map showing a contact's address? First, of course, you must have a street address in the person's entry (see page 157 for instructions on editing contacts). You also need to have some kind of maps app on your Fire. MapQuest is one decent option; see page 28 for how to install apps. Finally, tap the location marker icon (looks like a teardrop perched on its point) that appears next to any address in an open contact. It launches the maps app, and there you have it—a picture of your pal's postal address.

Typing Tips and Tricks

Even though it's just you tapping, the Fire can help you make text more quickly and accurately than you could on your own. For starters, there are the three biggies that every touchscreen typist nowadays expects: the Fire auto-inserts an apostrophe in common contractions (*I'm, Don't*); two taps of the space bar gets you a period; and you get auto-correct for common misspellings ("teh" gets changed to "the").

Keep an eye, as well, on the row above the traditional QWERTY keyboard. Here's where you get an ever-changing lineup of handy helpers. Before you start typing, this row sports a lineup of commonly used punctuation (exclamation point, question mark, @ sign, and so on). When you start typing, those guys disappear and in their place a horizontally swipeable row of auto-complete suggestions appear. So if you start typing the letters *raga*, what you see is: *raga*, *rags*, *ragamuffin*, and a dozen or so more. You'll notice that as you type, the word you're currently composing gets underlined. That's the Kindle's way of telling you: "Hey, if you choose to tap one of my auto-suggestions, this is what I'm gonna replace."

Even better: The spacebar also changes, temporarily, morphing into an "insert" button. As you type, then, if you like the Fire's leading suggestion (it gets highlighted in orange), all you need to do is tap the space/insert bar to pop it in your prose.

Sent from my Kindle Fire

CHAPTER 9

Browsing the Web

SILK—THE FIRE'S WEB BROWSER—IS Amazon's pride and joy. The app gets top-tier promotion on the Fire's product page, which proclaims it "revolution-ary." Silk even has its own website, with a slick, behind-the-scenes video from its makers (*http://amazonsilk.wordpress.com/*) and its very own Twitter account (@AmazonSilk).

Silk's mission boils down to two goals: making pages appear quickly and letting folks play Flash content (a notable omission from the iSomething-or-other). In its early days, though, the browser earned mixed reviews. Testers found that web pages on Silk loaded more slowly than on its competitors. Since then, things have improved considerably, thanks to some under-the-hood-tuning by Amazon's computer science PhDs. Combine that with some of the tips and tricks you'll read about in the pages ahead, and you'll soon be cruising the Web at a respectable (if not blazing) speed.

Visiting a Website

The first time you tap the home screen's Web link, you arrive at a page filled with a dozen shortcut icons. These lead to some of the Web's most popular sites, including Google, Facebook, and the Amazon-owned MyHabit (a fashion retailer). Tap any one of them to start your Web travels or, if you've got another destination in mind, use any of these methods:

- **Enter a web address.** Tap the oval where it says "Search or type URL" (the latter's a geekonym for "web address"—it stands for *universal resource locator*). Now enter *www.cnn.com*, *yahoo.com*, or whatever, and then tap Go (on the oval's right edge or the orange keyboard button). You don't need to type the *http://*—Silk fills it in for ya. And how's this for another timesaver: Perched atop the keyboard is an ever-changing list of sites that Silk *thinks* you're heading for. Start typing, for example, *www.reut* and—bingo—the list below suggests *www.reuters.com*, *www.reuters.com/finance/stocks* (one of the news site's most popular sections), and a few other pages from the Reuters family. Each gets a globe icon next to it, indicating it's a web page. Listings paired with a magnifying glass icon (for example, *www.reuters.com arabic*) indicate web searches that Silk is offering to carry out. (Two other icons you'll see at some point: a ribbon for sites in your Bookmarks collection and a clock for pages you've previously visited.)

TIP   Don't know the site's web address? Type *red cross*, *IHOP*, *state department*...to run a Google search. If what you're looking for is common enough, the first result is usually what you want. The note on page 181 has info on switching to Bing or Yahoo if you'd rather use those guys.

- **Use a bookmark.** Amazon starts you off with a dozen ready-to-tap short-cuts—the same ones you saw the first time you launched Silk. Tap the white ribbon on the Options bar and then tap any of the choices. Page 179 shows how to add your own.

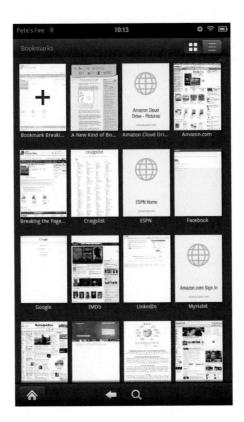

- **Head to a page you recently visited.** You can do this after you've surfed the Web a bit. At that point, when you launch Silk, a screen full of your latest stops online appears. It looks and works like the bookmark list: Tap any icon to head directly to that page. (If this icon-filled page doesn't appear, tap the upper-right corner's plus (+) button.) The History list offers a similar kind of breadcrumb trail, except here it's comprised of every web page you've viewed over the past month or so (or until the Fire fills up and starts flushing out old bits). To view it, on the Options bar, tap Menu→History.

Navigation and Viewing Basics

What to do when you land on a page? Perhaps you'd simply like to read a bit? Chances are the onscreen text is too small. Double-tap whatever looks good for a closer look. This gesture actually works for anything on the page, not just text: a picture, an ad, a video player. Once the page's content is a little more legible, place one finger on the screen and, as you hold it, move it around. The page sticks to your finger like a magnet. You can traverse, left, right, diagonal, wherever you like. You can also flick (page 25) the page in any direction. To zoom back out to full page view (or as much of it as will fit on the screen), double-tap again.

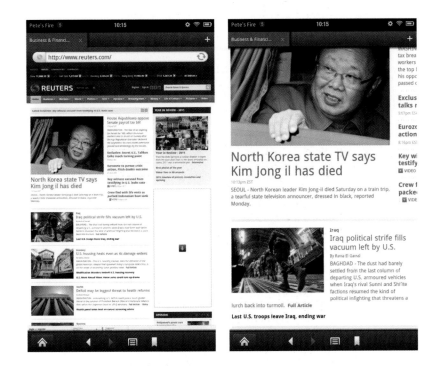

All it takes is a bit of practice: Double-tap anywhere to move in; repeat to move back out. To exert a bit more fine-tuned control, pinch and spread two fingers. The first zooms you in, the second zooms you out. What's the difference between this and the double tap? Pinching and spreading lets you stop exactly at whatever magnification level you prefer.

Following a link works just as you'd expect—tap it. The web address bar you met earlier drops from the top of the screen, to show where you're heading. A spinning circle on the left edge indicates that Silk is fetching the page you requested. Remember, you can click more than just the standard blue, underlined text. Most buttons, photos, and icons, when tapped, will transport you somewhere, or at the very least present an enlarged version of themselves.

TIP Accidentally tap a link you *don't* want to follow? You get a second or so in which to change your mind and issue a "stop!" command. In the web address oval, tap the right-hand "x" icon, which slides down from the top of the screen as Silk gets ready to fetch a linked page.

The Back arrow, in the Options bar, serves the same role as the one in your computer's web browser, returning you to the page you just came from. (If you've just launched Silk, tapping Back pops you back out to wherever on the Fire you came from.) To its right, the Forward arrow lights up and is ready for duty any time you've tapped Back. Prior to that, Forward appears on the Options bar but it's dimmed out.

One limitation to early web browsers—those of mid and late 90s—was how messy things got when you started clicking lots of links. Before you knew it, 15 separate web browser windows crowded your monitor, making navigation a mess. The solution? Tabbed browsing, which arranges multiple sheets in a single browser window with tappable tabs for easy navigation. Silk's got it from the start. Tap and hold any link and, in the pop-up list that appears, pick "Open in new tab." On top of the screen you've now got two rectangles—tap either one to view its web page. Add up to ten of these tabs, either via the tap-and-hold method or by touching the upper-right plus (+) button. That gets you a ready-for-your-command search/web address oval, and the recent-page miniatures described back on page 176.

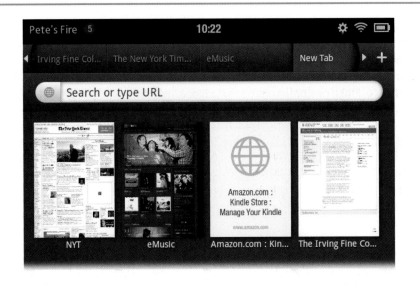

NOTE Every so often you'll run into a PDF or Word file posted on a website, ready for downloading. To do so, tap the link and Silk grabs the file off the Web and stashes it in its downloads folder. Head there (Options bar→Menu→Downloads) and then tap it again. A pop-up list shows all the apps on your Fire that can view it. Pick the one you want and now you're looking at it.

Favorites and Recently Visited Sites

Admit it, you have at least one or two websites you can't live without. You can save time and go straight to those spots by bookmarking them. First, use any of the techniques described back on page 174 to navigate to a favorite page. Then, on the Options bar, tap the Menu button and pick "Add bookmark." In the dialog box that pops up, tap OK to accept the suggested name and web address.

You'll probably leave the page address alone—you just picked it, after all. You may, however, wish to shorten the highlighted text in the Name box. Whatever you enter there shows up as a label beneath the page thumbnail on the Bookmarks screen. Really long titles, which is what you often get, only fit on one view of the Bookmarks' views (list view, when your Fire is held horizontally). Better to shorten things down so you can make out what's what when you're in, say, the Bookmarks' grid view. There you get about 16 characters max. So, rather than *Album | We Bought a Zoo (Motion Picture Soundtrack) | eMusic*, edit that down to something like *We Bought a Zoo*. To visit any of these favorite places, tap the white ribbon on the right side of the Options bar (that's where you can toggle, upper right, between grid and list view). Tap a bookmark to head to its page.

The History page (Options bar→Menu button→History) is like the Recents button on your cellphone. It shows a plain-text list of all the pages you've visited in the past month or so, split up into four categories: Today, Yesterday, "Last 7 days," and "Last month." Tap any item in one of these sections to pay it a return visit; the new page replaces whatever is currently in the frontmost tab.

Tap and hold any page name on the History list for a pop-up menu with a few related options. The first choice—Open—does the same thing as tapping an item in the History list. "Open in new tab" displays the page in a fresh tab; "Open in background tab" does the same but stashes the tab behind the currently visible one. "Share link" lets you email, tweet, or otherwise publicize the web address. "Copy link URL" sticks a copy of it on the clipboard. "Add bookmark" gives you a permanent shortcut to the page. Don't want everyone who uses your Fire knowing where you've been? Pick the final choice—Delete. In related news, the upper-right Clear All button does just as it says. Page 189 explains how to make your browsing totally breadcrumb free.

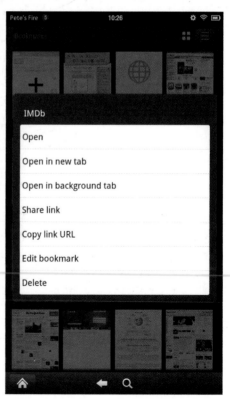

TIP   Instantly transform a page on the History list to a bookmark by tapping the gray button on the right edge of any link. You don't get any editing choices that way, but you can always tweak its particulars by opening Bookmarks, holding the newly added link's name, and then picking "Edit bookmark" from the pop-up menu.

Searching

What would the Web be if you couldn't search it? Silk is ready to play host to Google and its main competitors, and offers several search features of its own—right in the web address oval. You first met its finding powers at the start of this chapter (page 174), but it also has two other hunting tools:

- **Basic searches.** To recap guidance from earlier in this chapter: Tap any tab to summon the search oval and then touch the oval to start typing. The auto-suggest helper kicks in as soon as you hit the keyboard. Begin with *pe* and you're likely to see a list of recently visited pages that, somewhere in their title have those two letters. Tap ahead to *pepp* and suddenly all that history makes way for search suggestions: *pepperidge farm*, *peppa pig*, *pepperdine*, and so on. (The same list is horizontally swipeable across the top of the keyboard).

NOTE   To replace Google with either Bing or Yahoo, head to Options bar→Menu button →Settings →"Set search engine" to make your pick.

- **Search inside a page.** Sometimes you want to pinpoint a word or phrase on a (usually long) page. Use "Find in page" (Options bar→Menu), type your query into the search oval, and then tap the downward-pointing arrow, to the left of what you just typed. If it finds a match, Silk highlights it in orange. To find the next occurrence, tap the same arrow again. To reverse course, and return to an earlier match, touch the *upward*-pointing arrow. Readability tip: Dismiss the keyboard and free up more onscreen space by tapping its lower-right "hide" button. When you're finished, hit Done at the top right of the screen.

mally if a sequel shows up a mere two years after the original, w
importantly, Robert Downey r and Jude Law reprise their roles a
ginal, the team delivers one that is sure to keep the fans happy.

oyle loyalists dismissed the first film is that the frenetic pace an
hat does Mr. Ritchie do? He goes BIGGER and FASTER! There are
so elementary, my dear. Professor Moriarty is out to cause a wa
ur heroes can possibly stop him.

e first movie has been toned down here, and we get not only th
f third female character - a gypsy fortune teller, Madame Simza
doesn't last long, Reilly gets tossed from a moving train, and Ra
rld.

ed version that encourages discovery of Holmes by a new gener
arrow. Also, Professor Moriarty is very much a Bond-type villair
rackling chemistry between Downey and Law, make this a fun ti

Font and Other Appearance Adjustments

Amazon, no doubt, wants to make the Web as easy to read as ebooks. Just as
the Fire gives you all sorts of ways to customize a book's page (typeface choice,
font size controls, and so on), it offers a few ways to tailor your web experience,
too. But be prepared: Web pages are much less tameable than the ones in a
book. Read on for a select tour of your choices, grouped according to the kinds
of changes they make (how they're listed on the Fire is, frankly, a bit scatter-
shot). Get to these by following this path: Options bar→Menu→Settings.

- **Text size.** Five choices here, ranging from Tiny to Huge (yep, that's the label's name). As tempting as it is to bump up the factory-set middle size (Normal), given the Fire's smallish screen, proceed with caution if you do. Some sites look fine when Huge-ified. Others have been crafted to fit a more narrow range of magnification levels. In these cases, the really big text ends up making things look really awful.

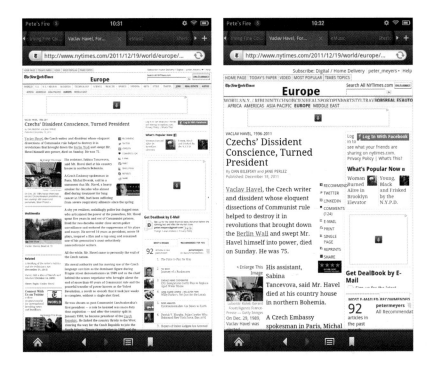

- **Auto-fit page.** Leave this on and, when you double-tap any text, the zoomed-in version automatically gets laid out anew to fit on the Fire's screen. Semi-related to the Auto-fit option is *Open pages in overview*, found in the Behavior section further down the Settings page. Leave this checkbox on and, each time a new page opens, you see as much as will reasonably fit into a bird's-eye view. When this setting is turned off, pages open automatically zoomed into the upper-left section of the page. The next item down also affects how things look. *Open in background,* when turned on, puts newly opened windows in a recessed tab. That is, the page you're currently viewing remains onscreen and the new page sits patiently behind it. Many web surfers like keeping this background setting as-is so they can focus on reading the page at hand and tack to-read links up on the tab bar, ready for reading when they're finished with the current page. On the other hand, if you want links you tap to launch pages that appear immediately, turn *Open in background* off.

- **Default zoom.** This setting controls what happens when you double-tap a spot on a web page. Close takes the area around where your finger hit and bumps it up nice and big. Medium and Far reduce the power of the zoom by a noticeable amount. The latter practically turns zooming off entirely—for eagle-eyes only. Most folks will want to test out Close or stick with the factory-set Medium.

- **Load images** and **Enable plug-ins.** (Plug-ins are helper programs embedded inside web pages that do things like play multimedia ads.) You can toggle these two separate settings on or off independently. Both strip away photos, ads, and other visual clutter. If picture overload is proving distracting, or your pages take too long to load, you may want to consider one of these. The first setting blocks photos and illustrations, the second nixes videos and Flash content. The plug-in setting actually has three variations: "Always on" (the default); "On demand" (sticks a tappable green arrow wherever a web page needs a plug-in's help); and Off. The underlying links behind all these outcast visuals still work—usually (depends on how the page was coded). So tap the big blank space to see what you would have missed. To be clear: You'd probably never turn this stuff off on a "real" computer, but to optimize space and speed, some people may want to test life on a text-only Web. If you're still unsure, start with *Enable plug-ins* set to "On demand"; many people find this setting provides a nice speed boost.

- **Desktop or mobile view.** Some websites present small-screen friendly versions of themselves when you visit using a mobile phone. Software-sniffing agents can detect what kind of hardware—PC or mobile phone—is behind the web browser used to view the site. But what makes sense for the Fire? The stripped-down, mainly text mobile version? Or the big kids' full view, multimedia-powered edition? If you do nothing, you'll get whatever the website decides. Some sites elect to trot out the mobile view for Fire-using visitors. To force them to show the regular desktop edition, pick "Desktop: Optimize for desktop view." The factory setting is "Automatic," which cedes the decision to the website; "Mobile" crunches sites into their mini versions if they're available.

TIP Want to block those annoying pop-up windows that used to clutter so many websites, and still spring up every so often? In the "Block pop-up windows" setting, take your pick between Ask (you get to decide each time one is ready to spring), Never, and Always.

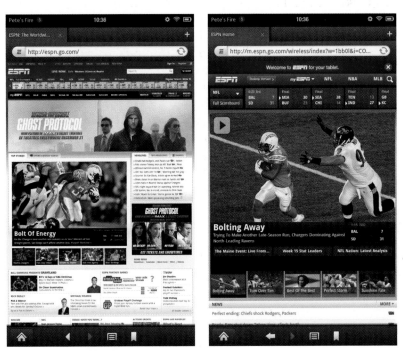

Desktop Version   Mobile Version

Copying Text and Images

To copy any text on a web page, hold your finger on the screen till you see two selection handles surround the word you've picked. To extend the selection, tap, hold, and move either handle to grab as much extra text as you want. When you're done, tap one of the handles. For about a second, a message will flash at the bottom of the screen: "Text copied to clipboard." Now it's sitting there for you to use in some kind of writing app (Email, for example; see page 166) where you then tap and hold any blank writing space and then pick Paste to grab what's on the clipboard.

Most web pages let you download and save pictures from them. Tap and hold the image you want till a pop-up list appears with choices to "Save image" or "View image." Choose the first and then switch over to the Gallery app (page 114) where it now awaits in the Download picture stack. The latter gets you a web page devoted exclusively to the image you're touching.

NOTE   Don't love the idea that all your downloaded images are saved in a list (or at least for the last month)? Head to Options bar→Menu button→Downloads and then put a checkmark next to any item you want to vanish; tap "Clear selection."

Sharing and Saving Web Pages

The Web is the most connected document library in human history, which may explain why folks want to share pages with each other so often. Doing so on the Fire is easy. Tap the "Share page" button (Options bar→Menu) and pick one of the apps on the pop-up list to send the web address to. The app choices that appear on your screen depend, of course, on which ones you've installed. At a minimum you'll see the Fire's built in "Send with Email." Now what about those cases when a simple link is not enough? Two good options for those who wish to grab everything that appears on a page from head to toe:

- **Web Snapshots.** This nifty li'l app (free or, without ads, for $1) does one thing: makes PDF replicas of any page you visit. Once you've downloaded it, the grabbing process works hand-in-hand with the Silk browser. Find a page you want and go through the "Share page" routine as described above. From the pop-up list, pick Web Snapshots. That launches the app, where you'll see your captured page. Tap the lower-right "Full PDF" button and, on the page that appears, tap the "view" radio button and the name of the page you just saved. Next, pick any PDF-viewing app on your Fire. Skip the Kindle Fire (it doesn't display Web Snapshot's PDFs very nicely) and go for something like the free Adobe Reader. You can also email the PDF by tapping the "share" button rather than the "view" button.

- **Read It Later Pro.** This $2.99 app gives you much more control over the web pages you save. And it teams up with a little utility button you can add to your regular computer's web browser, making it easy to spot and tag web pages at work that you don't have time to read. Later, call 'em up for perusing when you're at your Fire. Start by installing the app on your Fire. Create an account and come up with a user name and password. That's it: You're good to go. In the Fire's Silk browser, just follow the "Share page" instructions at the top of the page; in the list of share-friendly apps, you see Read It Later. Tap its name after copying any web page and then return to the app to read it even when you don't have a WiFi connection. To add a button to your regular computer's web browser (or iPhone, iPad, or other Android device), visit *http://ReadItLaterList.com*. Simple instructions are there for pinning Read It Later buttons on all your favorite web browsing tools. You'll find more than 100 apps that provide Read It Later options for Twitter, RSS readers, and so on.

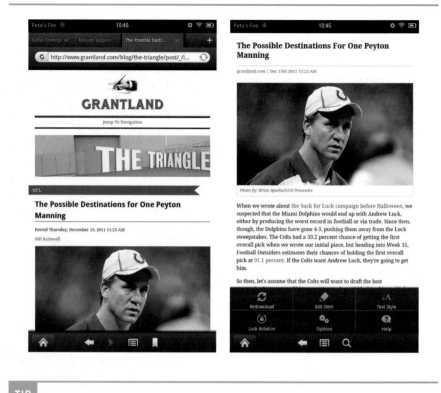

For really quick page sharing, tap and hold a site's *favicon*—the tiny, branded icon on the left edge of the web address bar—for a pop-up list with three choices: Copy, Paste, and "Share page."

Security and Other Advanced Settings

Most people can have a long and happy relationship with their Fire without ever reading this section. For some, however, an opportunity to fine-tune some of the more obscure corners of their latest gadget is too strong to resist. If that sounds like you, in Silk, head to Settings (Options bar→Menu) and check out these options:

- **Saved Data.** The first two items— *Accept cookies* and *Clear all cookie data*—have nothing to do with snacks. Cookies are small record-keeping text files that websites deposit on a computer any time you visit them. They hold, for example, your user name and certain browsing activity on a site like Amazon.com. They also help some Internet advertising firms serve up ads that match the sorts of sites you've visited. If the intrusiveness of the latter outweighs the convenience of the former, you may want to remove the checkbox from "Accept cookies" and, for good measure, hit "Clear all cookie data." (That's also one way to flush out all cookie-tracked info without permanently forbidding the use of cookies.)

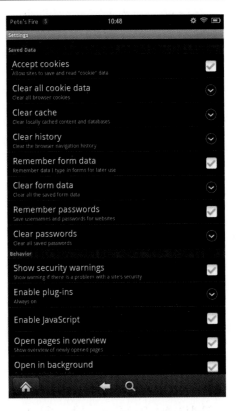

In related news, *Clear cache* and *Clear history* empty out items that web publishers frequently use (logos, for example) and all the web pages you've visited over the past month or so, respectively. When *Remember form data* is turned on, many sites will retain personal info you've entered into other sites (name, address, phone number, and so on). Even when turned on, this service doesn't always work—its success depends on consistent form design, something that doesn't always happen. The *Remember passwords* checkbox does the same thing but focuses only on user names and passwords. Especially if you've got a media-hungry kid borrowing your Fire, you may want to leave this option turned off. If you're especially cautious, tap the next item—*Clear passwords*—prior to sharing your Fire with anyone you don't fully trust.

- **Behavior.** If you leave the *Show security warnings* checkbox on, Silk will raise a flag (actually, throw up a message window) if you're about to visit a website whose behind-the-scenes documentation looks fishy or non-existent. Page 184 has the scoop on how to decide about the *Enable plug-ins* choices. *Enable JavaScript* is a checkbox that the vast majority of people will want to leave turned on, since so many sites today use JavaScript technology to beef up their interactivity. It's also a tool used by some miscreants to do harm, but by disabling it, you're depriving yourself of most of what's pleasing on the Web today.

- **Advanced.** *Accelerate page loading* is the marquee option here. Amazon has put a ton of engineering effort into making Silk as fast as possible. Part of this effort involves using some of the company's enormous fleet of servers to handle behind-the-scenes page building that happens each time you view a web page. While in theory this approach should make pages load faster, in practice, especially in the Fire's early days, this didn't always seem to be the case. Amazon did not quite go so far as to verify these claims, but did admit that Silk's performance would at least partially depend on more people using it more often. So where does all this leave you, someone who may be reading this a month or a year after the Fire launched? If you're unhappy with the Silk browser's speed, try turning off this setting and see if it makes a difference. If not, flip it back on—long term, it should speed things up. Finally, there's *Reset to default*. Fiddled with things so much that you wished for the Silk you met first time out of the box? Here's your path back to the way things were.

Kindle in Appland

CHAPTER 10

Playing Games

YOU DON'T HAVE TO be a Doritos-munching, Red Bull–chugging teenager to cheer the news: The Fire is one wicked fun gaming machine. Whether you're into angry avians or you just like your morning Sudoku, the Fire is ready to frolic. The device's easily graspable size is a big factor here. You can pull it out of a shoulder sling or pocketbook any time the mood strikes. And thanks to the hard work of developers worldwide, the range of titles in Amazon's Appstore for Android is already decent, even in the Fire's early days. Dozens and dozens of choices await (yes, including Angry Birds) in categories like arcade, educational, racing, and sports. In fact, selection overload is precisely the problem that stumps some fans eager to get their game on. Where to start? That's what this chapter is designed to help you with. Consider it your own guided tour of the Appstore's recreational aisles.

NOTE A handful of the app profiles in this and the following two chapters are based on reviews written by yours truly in the recent book *Best iPad Apps* (O'Reilly). All apps in these chapters have been re-tested on the Fire, and operational descriptions have been tweaked accordingly, but if you've perused that earlier work, you may recognize some highlights and shout-outs.

Making Shapes

Touchscreens mean you no longer have to mess with menus and mice to indicate what you want to put *right here*. The intimate connection the following apps offer between finger and object-under-construction make it easy to unleash your inner builder.

- **Doodle Fit ($0.99).** This charming little shape puzzler separates the world, more or less, between those who pack luggage in a car trunk efficiently.... and those who don't. Your job is to fill the oddly configured, empty geometric shapes with smaller component blocks (also oddly configured). Do so by dragging the latter into the former. Sounds easy, and at first it is. But soon these increasingly intricate visual challenges make you realize that playing with blocks isn't always so simple. The hand-drawn canvas and shapes add to the game's apparent simplicity, but don't let that fool you. With 100-plus levels, you can spend hours in DoodleLand.

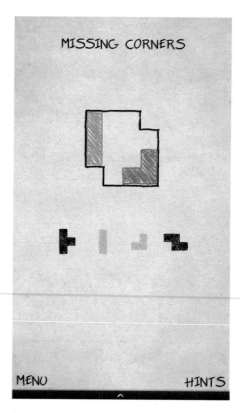

- **X Construction ($1.49; free Lite version).** Calling all wanna-be and real-life civil engineers. Build the bridges your people need so their trains can cross chasms, gulleys, and other gaps safely. The app starts off each test supplying you with a fixed number of steel girders, concrete struts, and supporting cables. You need to figure out how to assemble them in a sufficiently sturdy way. If you build the bridge incorrectly, the test train that crosses tumbles off the rickety structure. The ensuing screams—and they do really seem like they're coming from *inside* the falling train—are disturbingly amusing. The paid version is ad free, offers ten more levels (25) than the free edition, and gives you a dozen "sandbox" testing areas to practice your bridge-building skills.

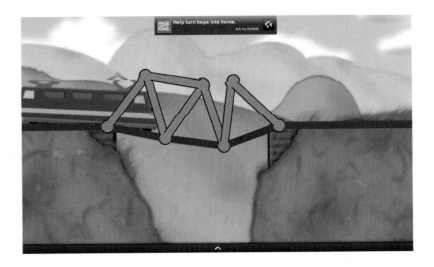

Finding Paths

Path finding has been a common theme in video games ever since the first version of Pong. The central task so often comes down to mentally calculating trajectories and doing so quickly. That's what these games offer, except here they're updated with 21st-century sights and sounds.

- **Quell ($0.99).** Probably a fitting choice, this game's minimalist name, but you could just as well call it *Gobble the Bubbles While Listening to Soothing Music*. Whatever its title, the game's challenge lies in figuring out how to push your one precious blue bubble around the board so it sops up all the gold nibblets in sight. In your way are various mortal obstacles (sharp-toothed counter-gobbly creatures; green dots that morph into impassable blocks; endless, inescapable loops). The Winter Hill-style soundtrack makes it almost easy to forget about these threats; it's easy to imagine you're about to settle in for a nice long massage. The 80-plus challenge levels offer enough variety for many, many hours of path-finding entertainment. Or bring it out for breaks between (during?) conference calls, on the train home, or while waiting for the kids.

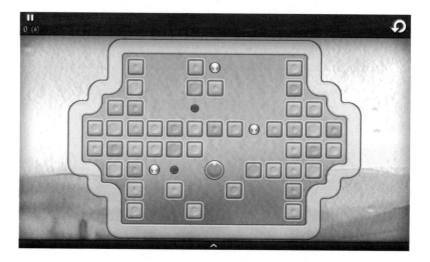

- **Cut the Rope ($0.99).** Amazon's Appstore is loaded with so-called *physics games*, which invite you to replicate real-world actions: Pull a slingshot back and release it; bolt together sturdy bridges; squeeze air from a balloon at a rope-dangled lollipop, causing the candy to swing in a certain direction so that when you cut said rope its sugary charm drops into the mouth of a waiting frog. Sounds ridiculous, true. But this wildly popular game has taken off for reasons that are as clear as they are charming. You really end up exercising your noggin trying to plan out how and when to cut the rope. Prior to feeding the frog, you need to rack up points. Do so by moving the dangling candy into the yellow stars—using balloon-pushed air, altitude-boosting bubbles, or other similarly silly methods. Spiked barriers that you need to navigate your shiny red circle around often protect the frog; unending descents are what'll kill ya. If you send your circle southward and it misses the frog's target mouth, it's game over.

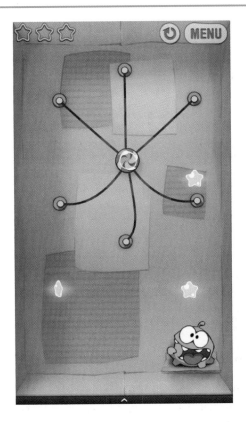

- **Paper Toss (free).** This app stages its namesake activity every place you've ever imagined doing it: Waiting in an airport, hangin' at a bar, and, of course, in your office cubicle. The variables that separate champs from chumps are distance and wind speed (the latter controlled by a fan whose direction and velocity are represented by onscreen labels that change with each throw). For fan speeds under 1.00 or so, aim head on. More than 4.00, and it's time to summon your inner geometer. Like golf putters who aim up-slope, you must flick your trash drastically off course (or so it would seem). Then watch as the breeze catches your shot and curves it right into the receptacle.

Falling Objects

The Fire's not 3D (yet...give it time), so in these games the objects won't make you duck. What they will do is fill you with the same anxiety that *I Love Lucy's* star had watching all those chocolate cherries speed past her on the candy factory's conveyor belt. Hurry up and catch 'em!

- **180 Ultra ($0.99; free basic version).** A cascade of multicolored coins descend slowly and in columns down your screen. From your own little change purse you pull similarly-shaped discs, trying to build out patterns—three across, four down—that zap away the coordinated coins and earn you points. All this starts getting harder as the colors and speed increase *and* you try to keep any column from descending too low and ending the game. A bunch of different play modes give you different ways to test out your tapping skills. Endless, for example, pushes you to go for as long as you can live. Score-, Time-, and Drop Attack mode pit you against fixed limits (250 matches to win, max number of matches in 90 seconds). There's also another motivator, on the free version, that may make you keep practicing: If you successfully finish enough levels, the ads go away.

- **Fruit Ninja ($0.99; free basic version).** The object here is deceptively simple: Finger-swipe your sword through each banana, strawberry, and other fruit salad ingredient that some unseen juggler is tossing in front of you. If you clank on one of the randomly appearing bombs, your ninjaness is no more. Wanna pimp out your sword collection? Visit the Dojo to select new styles, more of which become available the more you play.

Quizzes and Brain Teasers

Rest your fingers. Time to exercise your mind. Video games meet education in these brain-building apps.

- **The Secret of Grisly Manor ($0.99).** This app is one of the best examples of what some predicted would happen to novels in the Computer Age: They'd turn into audience-piloted explorations of richly illustrated worlds. Behind each door, and within each room, users could inspect objects, chew on clues ("There's something hidden underneath the grate"), and decide how to navigate the storyline. Needless to say, Stephen King still has a job. But the puzzle adventures on display in Grizzly Manor are still a remarkable achievement in interactive entertainment. The heart of the story revolves around a letter from your dear old grandad, pleading for help to come rescue him. His mansion is chock full of questions, clues and, perhaps, grandpa himself.

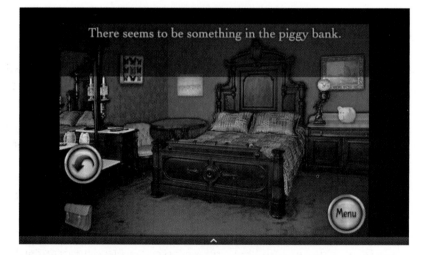

- **Monkey Preschool Lunchbox ($1.99).** A large part of guilt-free ownership of a gadget like the Fire lies in justifying its usefulness. If you've got toddlers in your life, one way down this path is with apps like this one, a collection of fun but challenging tasks. A half-dozen activities are included: color matching (tap all the green fruit), simple jigsaw puzzles, Concentration-style memory games. The game cycles through variations of all these and rewards players with virtual sticker selections each time they get a few in a row right. No good deed goes entirely unpunished: For example, the game has no built-in "kill the annoying music" option. But you're helping educate the world's next generation if that makes you feel any better.

Word Puzzlers and Number Boards

Word lovers have fallen in love with the touchscreen editions of their favorite board- and paper-based games. The best part of these digital versions are the worldwide matches they provide when you're looking for a partner.

- **Scrabble (Kindle Fire Edition) ($2.99).** The competition in this category is slim: Hasbro's lawyers made sure only one app gets to use its eight-letter moniker. But the company justifies this solo slot. The number of playing options is huge: against the computer, by yourself (odd, but possible), "pass and play" with up to three other competitors (opponents' racks are hidden between turns), against Facebook friends, or matched up with random opponents.

  Three types of game styles are on offer: classic (the play-till-you're-finished mode of yore), point-based (first to reach 75 or 150 points wins), or a fixed number of rounds. The Shuffle button is a helpful way of juggling the letters in your rack, if you're having a hard time envisioning words. You can also consult an in-app dictionary. Those in search of greater aid can tap the heart-shaped Best Word button. The app software-magically figures the highest-scoring play for your current board.

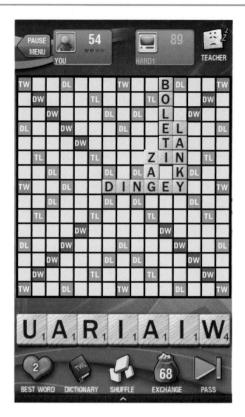

- **Words with Friends (free).** Credit John Mayer for much of this Scrabble knockoff's skyrocketing popularity. Back in 2009 the rocker tweeted, "Words with Friends app is the new Twitter." Traffic exploded. Good news for the developers (since scooped up by gaming giant Zynga) and good news for those not ready to shell out for the official Scrabble app. Beyond the no-brainer price, the main lure of this no-nonsense app—you won't find nearly as many gaming options as in Scrabble—is found in the "Friends" part of the title. More than 20 million people have accounts. In an instant, any one of them can be tapping tiles with you. And with a recently added Facebook option, you can now reach them on The Social Network, other Android devices, and anyone using an iPad or iPhone.

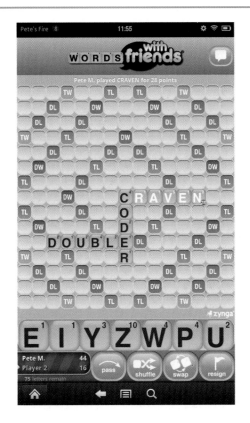

- **Enjoy Sudoku ($2.99; free Daily version).** Facing a hugely crowded category, this app excels by offering maximum variety and, for Sudoku newcomers, a little bit of hand-holding. You get more than a dozen difficulty levels, several tutorial lessons, and a healthy dose of in-game hints, some of which link to in-depth lessons on the Sudoku reference guide site (*http://Sudopedia.org*). Most edifying is the way hints unfurl from slightly cryptic, gentle reminders to a detailed explanation of why, say, a 6 goes in the 8th row, cell 1. The graphics won't win any app art awards, but for turning your puzzling hobby into a mind-improving habit, you can't do much better. The paid version is ad-free, offers an unlimited number of variations (as opposed to the freebie edition's one per day), and gives you more practice games to hone your craft.

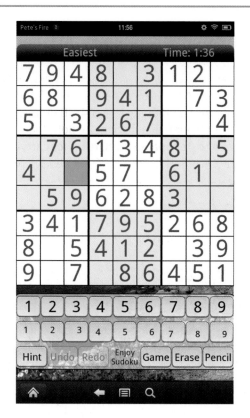

Driving and Flying

Up, up, and away! Or: Vroooooom. Take your pick. When you have the need for speed, check out either of these apps.

- **Asphalt 6: Adrenaline (Kindle Fire Edition) ($6.99).** For old-school purists looking to log serious hours behind the virtual wheel, this app is worth its above-market-average price. The graphics alone are stunning, proof that the Fire is capable of riding alongside, if not quite exceeding, the iPad and Sony's PSP. What you get in Asphalt 6 is plenty: dozens of car and track options (more of which open up as you rack up victories), escalating racing challenges (some races cut the laggard after each heat), and multiplayer options (either against online opponents or other Fire-owning pals).

Your Fire serves as a steering wheel—tilt it in the direction you want to turn. Acceleration is managed automatically by the app in the factory-set steering mode. Or, to handle acceleration (and other controls like braking) manually, switch by opening up the onscreen Options menu. One size-able downside is worth noting. After the app's initial 2.4 MB download, the opening screen informs you that *another* 514 MB of graphics need to come on down to make this thing fully functional. Oddly, there's no mention of *that* on the game's Appstore page. If you're up for carrying such a big load, by all means spend the money, and the 20 minutes it takes to download those extras. Then grab your driving gloves and hit the track.

- **My Paper Plane 2 (3D) ($1.98, free Lite version).** One thing that racing newbies may not like about Asphalt 6 is how fast those darn cars move. For a more leisurely ride, lose the engine and take to the sky. That's right, a plane-flying app—okay a *paper* plane game, but still—is one way to steer the Fire in a more leisurely manner. This app couldn't be simpler to operate. As in Asphalt, you tilt left and right to steer and move the Fire toward and away from you to control altitude. But because you're not riding in a nitro-powered vehicle, the trip unfolds in a way that many, novices especially, will find easier, and more pleasurable to control. (Gaming vets will want to pass wide of this app for that very reason.) The free version is the way to start. You get a helpful tutorial and one terrain to play around with (the object is to collect stars scattered around an obstacle course). With the paid edition, you get three more landscapes to soar across.

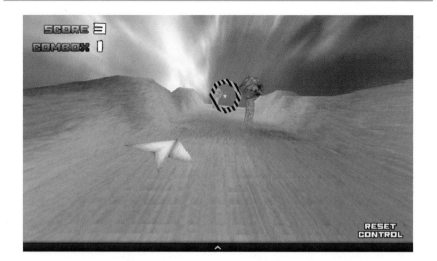

One thing a chapter on app games *doesn't* need is a write-up of Angry Birds. That's old news by now to pretty much everyone. The only extra advice worth sharing is about all the various editions in Amazon's Appstore. No fewer than five different Fire-compatible versions exist. They range from totally free with ads (Angry Birds Seasons Free) to cheap—$0.99—with just a few ads (Angry Birds Ad-Free; Angry Birds Rio Ad-Free; Angry Birds Seasons Ad-Free). The latter trio are thematic variations on the original concept—good for anyone whose addiction needs multiple outlets. For serious fans, there's also a version that's specially made just for the Fire and comes with a price to reflect that fact: Angry Birds HD Kindle Fire Edition ($4.99). The graphics are better, but not spectacularly so, compared to the regular editions.

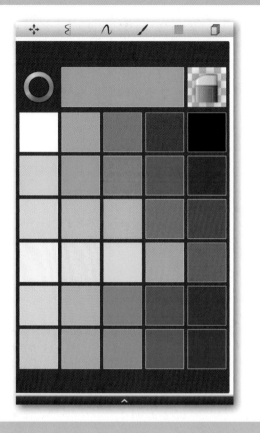

CHAPTER 11

Creative Corner

THE PUNDITS AGREE: the Fire's sole job is to serve as vending machine for Amazon's digital merchandise. And plenty of people will, no doubt, step up and start buying. Between movies and music and ebooks and TV, the tap-and-shop allure of this device is pretty compelling. And yet...in every class there's that kid who can't stop drawing. And in conference rooms worldwide, while meetings are underway, amateur and professional doodlers alike work at their art. Add in the singers and songwriters among us and it's clear: Artists will use the tools at hand to make what they love. Is the Fire the best canvas for all these endeavors? Of course not. But its appeal as an always-handy, surprisingly powerful, multi-media playpen is just starting to come into focus. This chapter rounds up a few of the most promising tools that creative types will want to check out.

Painting and Drawing

Quick: What do you get when you put a touchscreen in front of someone who likes to draw, sketch, or paint? Someone who will figure out a way to get this new kind of sketchbook to work—no matter what the pundits say. Some of the tools in this realm are basic, some are already seriously powerful. All are guaranteed to lead to some really fun results.

- **Text Picture (Ascii Art) (free).**
  This one won't win any prize for encouraging originality—it's essentially a collection of alpha- and numeric-character drawings that you can grab and use. But for free, who's complaining? You can create your own so-called "Ascii art" (named for the keyboard symbols that some early computer artists used to make these digital figurines), but don't expect any help. All you get is a blank canvas. The main attraction, for most people, is the depth of the premade choices: dozens of ready-to-use—or, perhaps, modify—Ascii art models spread out across categories like People, Romance, and Vehicles. At a minimum, it'll put a :) on your face.

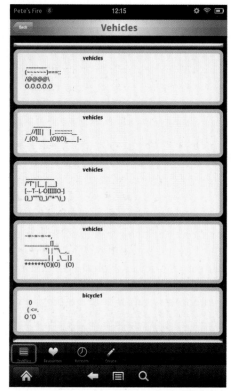

- **Drawing Pad ($1.99).** This delightfully usable, kid-friendly app is a creativity-encouraging vortex from which your child may not soon emerge. The app's designer made the brilliant decision to forgo options you'd find in painting programs for grownups: separating color choices in a different toolbox, layers (a concept many *adults* don't understand), and brush size controls. Instead, Drawing Pad shows the tool as-is: Paint it or leave it. The main choices include paint brushes, colored pencils, crayons, markers, pattern stamps, stickers, and paper. The stickers are especially fun for the little ones. They can resize and rotate any of these guys by pinching, spreading, and twisting their fingers.

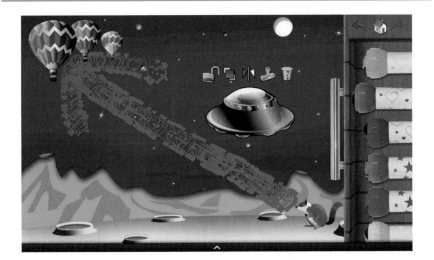

- **Sketchbook Mobile ($1.99; free Express version).** AutoDesk, the firm behind this drawing and painting app, is the same company that sells high-powered 3D, animation, and design tools. So no surprise that what you get here is something much more than a simple sketchpad with a few pen and brush choices. You get: 40-plus different brush shapes, each with fully customizable settings like opacity, radius, and splatter effects; layers (virtual, transparent sheets that you can position different elements of your drawing on); blend modes (to control how adjacent layers combine with each other); and the ability, in the paid version, to export in popular file formats, including JPEG, PNG, and the Photoshop-ready PSD (with any layers you've created still intact). They've also, thankfully, equipped this app with 20 levels of undo/redo so no matter how much you experiment, you can always get back to where you started.

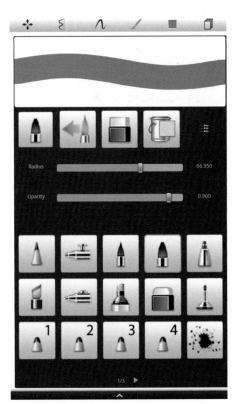

- **Skitch (free).** This one's for adults who don't have time to learn all that's under the hood of an app like Sketchbook Mobile. Drop-dead simple, this app comes from the Evernote (page 229) family. Skitch makes it easy for the artistically average to add arrows, lines, circles, and text to existing images and photos. But don't just waste your time drawing antlers on your college roommate's baby—the app's got business and design value as well. You can mark up the changes you want to see on the next version of your website or point out something a competitor is doing well. In scenarios like this you'll want to Skitch in tandem with Evernote's ability to grab and save web page snapshots. Drawing dropouts will especially like the auto-align services wired into Skitch's simple tool collection. They gently nudge your slightly squiggly lines straight (a setting that you can disable if you don't want that). Other nice touches: The typographical tools are fun to play with and it's intuitive to select, move, and stretch any lines or shapes you've created.

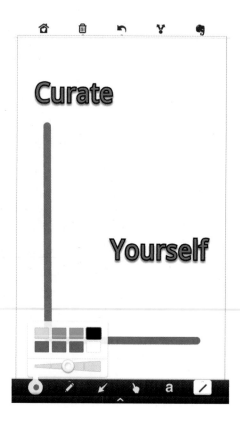

Photos

Would you really want to edit photos on the Fire? The answer's probably no, given the wealth of options available on a regular computer with a larger screen. And yet, again, there's being able to touch the thing you want to tweak that offers a concrete, common-sense appeal.

- **PicSay Pro ($3.99).** This app lets you do things like add word balloons and stickers to any photos you've got stashed in your Gallery app. (PicSay Pro creates duplicate copies so your originals stay intact.) The word balloons let you turn fun pictures into hysterical cartoons; the stickers let you add hats, hairstyles, beards, and so on to your pals and frenemies' mugs. Use various tap, pinch, and spread gestures to get everything looking just how you like. And for less frivolous editing, there's a fully stocked Effects menu that lets you adjust photos along every dimension you'd expect: exposure, saturation, tint, and red-eye fixes (to name just a few). A couple dozen filters, frames, and distortion effects (neon, rainbow) add up to a seriously fun way to get more for $4 than a mere cup of coffee. Photo fans will end up spending loads of time playing with this thing.

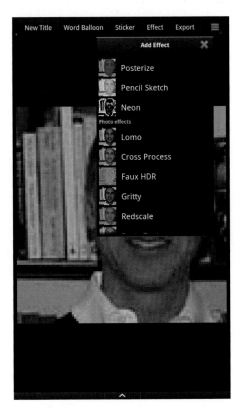

Music

You can play thousands of pro-quality tunes on the Fire, right? So why not use this machine's musical talents to compose some of your own sweet sounds? Well, app makers in this department aren't quite as far along as their visual art counterparts, but a few examples exist to show where things are heading.

- **Little Piano Pro ($0.99; free basic version).** To be sure, this app isn't a real instrument or even a halfway decent digital replica of one. What it is, though, is great for two- to four-year olds who will love how mom and dad's new toy is now an interactive entertainment machine for them. To be fair, this thing could conceivably occupy adults who either a) know it's not a full-fledged piano (you can't hold a note, the range is only one octave, and so on), or b) just love the idea of tapping a screen and getting it to play *something* that resembles music. Instrument choice goes beyond the piano: You get faux trumpet, guitar, bells, and percussion. You can load up a dozen or so pre-programmed songs (Jingle Bells, Oh Susanna!), and tap the keys as they light up. Suddenly, you're playing...okay, not really playing, but still having fun.

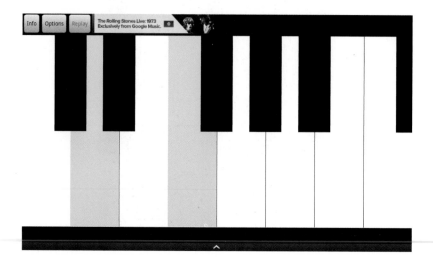

- **Chordbot Pro ($1.99).** If you have more serious musical needs, this app could come in handy. Thousands of fans have already given it four- and five-star rankings (on the Android Market). Chordbot does one thing really well—play a hugely customizable collection of piano and synthesizer chord progressions. You'll need some musical background to get any use out of this app. But for its intended audience—songwriters interested in doing a little bit of experimenting or soloists looking for some accompaniment—it's an incredible example of what the Fire can do. It works by letting you pick from a list of chords, selecting a tempo, and then hitting Play. After that, it's showtime.

Cooking and the Kitchen

Smartphones are too small to prop up and read across the kitchen, but the Fire's 7-inch screen is just about big enough. Prop 'er up against the toaster, dial up your favorite recipe, and get cooking with these apps.

- **Allrecipes.com DinnerSpinner for Android (free).** Gourmet chefs and those who can saunter confidently into the kitchen and whip up a meal, move along. For the rest of us food soldiers, though, facing five empty tables a week, this one's a no-brainer. Stocked with 40,000 dishes from the volunteer brigades at this popular website, it's perfect for finding your next meal. Start either by browsing the top-10, highly rated "featured" recipes or give the DinnerSpinner a twirl. The latter is an incredibly helpful way to tap choices in three big categories: type of meal (appetizer, soup, main), ingredients (from beef or cheese to shellfish or vegetable), and time available. There's also a traditional search tool. Once you've found a good match, either read it on your Fire or email it to yourself to print. Bon appetit.

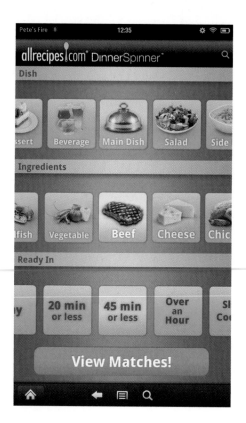

- **Jamie's 20 Minute Meals ($7.99).** Are crowdsourced recipes, like those in the Allrecipes app, always crowd pleasers? The thing is, you never know. Even with ratings and comments, you just can't be sure that what satisfies one cook is going to work for you. For a nearly surefire collection, consider springing for this relatively pricey entry from British super-cook Jamie Oliver. The catalog here's not huge—60 recipes, spread out across common categories like soups, pasta, stir-fry, and curries. But his skills as an engaging teacher work well with the multimedia talents that a digital cookbook offers.

Each recipe starts with a two-tabbed list of the ingredients and equipment you'll need (at the tap of a button you can save and, later, email the list). Next comes nicely illustrated step-by-step instructions. The app also includes two dozen or so short-to-medium length videos (they top out at around 10 minutes) giving visual tutorials on topics that aren't always easy to explain in prose: preparing an avocado, chopping an onion, what to look for when buying fish. This app costs more than most, but for those looking to cook well, and quickly, it's a good deal.

- **Kitchen Unit Converter ($0.99, basic version free).** Plenty of all-purpose conversion apps can be found in the Appstore. But if you're looking for one that focuses on cooking-related tasks, here's the one you want. Three conversion tabs let you pick between Volume, Weight, and Temperature. Whatever you select controls the choices that appear on the "convert from" and "convert to" wheels on either side of the screen. When you've got everything set just right, tap Convert, and the info you need shows up in the Results box. No muss, no fuss. A simple app for a simple task. (Free version comes with ads; paid version slices those off.)

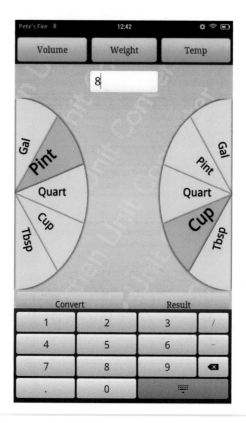

- **Chef's Kitchen Timer (free).** Keeping track of multiple stove-top pots, pans—not to mention what's in the oven—is most definitely not a simple task. Most kitchens top out at two or three timers. Throw in a cellphone and maybe you've got one more. This app stands out among a bunch of competitors. Set as many clocks a-tickin' as you like. The app doesn't have to be running to ring off—your Fire can be fast asleep and the chimes will ring. Pick from half a dozen different ring styles in the Preferences menu, which is also where you can designate how long these fellas keep chirping once they go off.

> **TIP** To change the label from New Timer to the name of whatever dish you're tracking, tap the time once you've set it and type in a name for this clock.

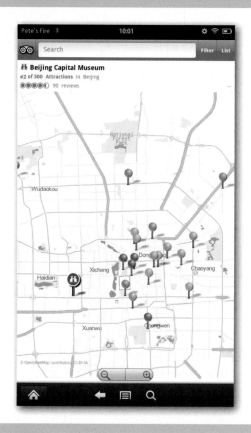

CHAPTER 12

Managing Time, Tasks, and Travel

WHEN IT COMES TIME to hit the road, your Fire, of course, is coming along for the ride. Why not put it to work? Beyond its ebook, music, and video collections, Amazon's newest Kindle offers thousands of apps that can help when you're away from home. The first big bucket under review in this chapter—clocks and calendars—are tools that will help regardless of how far, or not, your travels take you. Turning your Fire into a reliable appointment minder is something that can boost it from fun gadget into essential assistant. Further ahead, you'll meet some reliable to-do list helpers, general-purpose notetakers, and itinerary tracking tools. You'll also see how to find the best places to chow and bed down. And, finally—because somehow you'll need to pay for all these adventures— you'll get the latest on mobile bookkeeping tools for the Fire. The best way to truly enjoy your time away from home is to know, with a tap and a swipe, that there's money in the bank for when your return.

Clocks and Calendars

Forget about struggling with hotel clock radios. Turn to your Fire for wake-up and timekeeping duties. Then, once you're up, rely on it as a schedule minder throughout your event-packed days.

- **Alarm Clock Xtreme ($1.99; basic version free).** Wake yourself up or keep yourself honest. An alarm clock app is a great way to remind you to get up and stretch or check on the baby. This attractive, easy-to-operate tool does all the basics and more. It lets you set multiple alarms for different times, schedule ones that repeat (every weekday morning, for example), and greets you with either a silent blinking screen, a dozen-plus ringtones, or any music stored on your device. A typical snooze feature is included, whose duration you can customize anywhere from one to 60 minutes. Best of all, Xtreme stays on duty even when your Fire's asleep. Free version has ads; paid version doesn't.

- **Cozi Family Organizer (free).** Keep the family in sync with this attractively priced, simple to use app. Make and view appointments either in the app or on a linked, web-based account. The company's servers keep everything coordinated. These multiple entry points also make this app a good option for letting all family members add events from all kinds of devices (other Fires, mobile phones, web-connected computers). You do, however, need a live WiFi connection to see any of Cozi's data, so if you want a calendar that works on, say, long car drives, consider a higher-powered alternative (like CalenGoo, covered next).

Cozi offers limited integration with calendars stored in Outlook, Google, and Windows Live. Don't expect the changes you make in any of these calendaring programs to make their way into Cozi with great speed. Cozi works best when everyone in your group uses it as a shared, web-based calendar. One especially nice touch: Irregular appointments (taking Spot to the vet) appear in bold to help distinguish them from recurring events. The app also includes a few other digital family helpers that you can share among your team—lists for things like tasks and shopping, and a journal. The ads are persistent but fairly unobtrusive; if they really bother you, a $5 per month Gold account gets rid of 'em.

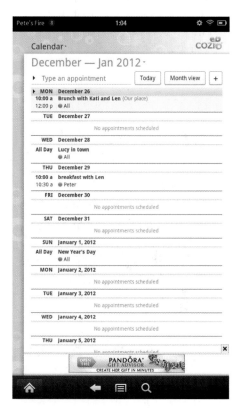

- **CalenGoo ($5.99).** The go-to option for folks who want their Fire to serve as a portable daybook. You get full-fledged integration with Google Calendar, there are no ads, and everything's viewable whether or not you're online. Syncing, of course, only happens when you have a live Internet connection. But when you are hooked up, the changes made in either direction (from Web to Fire, or vice versa) happen instantaneously. Reminders even work when the Fire is asleep. You get lotsa ways to speedily enter appointments and tasks, and a nice search tool for hunting down when you did what.

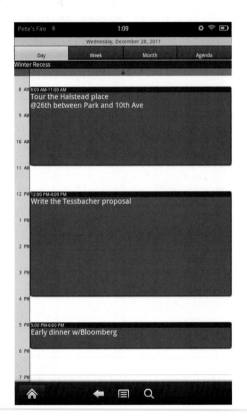

To-Do Lists and Notes

"Getting things done" is a mantra for many people today. Whether you follow the rigid methodology of a professional task-slaying guru (like David Allen, the brains behind the so-called GTD movement) or just want a way to digitally jot down your lists, these apps will help you stay on track.

- **ColorNote Notepad Notes (free).** The only thing overdone in this app is its repetitively redundant name. Much more importantly, it's a great bare-bones listmaker, providing a sheaf of virtual paper on which to capture reminders, to do lists, and random ideas. You can create two kinds of lists: checklists and plain notes. The first come with a gratifying feature: Swipe any item and it gets crossed off. Plain notes look like a big yellow pad stuffed onto your Fire. A built-in sharing tool makes it simple to append any list to an outgoing email.

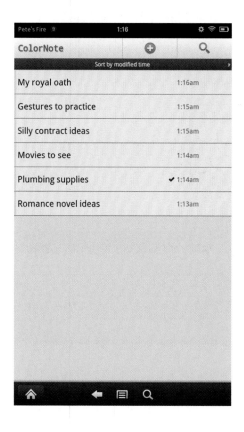

- **Out of Milk Pro ($4.99; basic version free).** An app dedicated to supermarket shopping is one way to justify bringing your Fire out and about on your daily errands. This specialized utility sets its sights on everything you might want to get at the grocery store. An auto-suggest list built around common supermarket items means that you can usually get what you want by tapping the first couple of letters. Quantity and unit fields make it easy to specify amounts. Simple email sharing is available for everyone, but for real shopping power, spring for the Pro version. That creates a web-based record of everything you type on the Fire. You can edit and add in both directions and—for some serious household efficiency—partner up with a mate and take advantage of real-time list sharing: *Rocky Road, 1 pint, stat!*

- **Evernote (free).** Evernote's much more than a souped-up notes app. With it you can capture any idea worth saving (like a web page snapshot, audio note-to-self, photo, or essay outline), group these into searchable collections, and sync the whole schmeer, automatically, among pretty much every device known to gadgetkind. But this app's real power lies in how it coordinates with other Team Evernote players: desktop software, a web-based version and browser plug-in, and lots of different smartphone and tablet apps. All of them are free, and all are ready to take a multimedia memo whenever the whim hits. Speaking of coordination: The app's "shared notebooks" feature lets you and one or more pals contribute to and view a common collection of notes. As you move through your digital day, grabbing and adding, the service is both scribe and personal library.

Shell out for the premium version ($5/month or $45/year) and you get extras like the ability to attach and sync video, Word and Excel files, more storage, and no ads. Either way, though, your stuff is yours to keep. The PC and Mac programs both let you export what you've input either as HTML files or a geek-friendly XML package.

TIP Want a to-do tool, but don't like the industry-wide convention for listing everything in, uh, lists? Check out Taskpad (*http://amzn.to/sDVK7E*). It lets you organize items in customizable quadrants. Change the size of the sectors that hold more important tasks for a quick visual reminder of what deserves more attention.

Dining Out

No matter how much you love your Fire, at some point, you gotta eat. Find the best spot for noshing, using a pioneer in the food-finding field.

- **Urbanspoon (free).** About five years ago, Urbanspoon began its quest to add slot-machine-style fun to the chore of restaurant picking. Not sure where to eat? Click the Spin button and get a randomly selected recommendation. The service started on the iPhone, where its popularity exploded (you could shake to spin). Now's your chance to whirl the famous wheel on the bigger screen. Truth is, the fancy finding mechanism is only a small part of what makes this app a winner. It's really the huge database of listings this service draws from that makes it a useful tool. About 800,000 restaurants are covered, and not just in big cities: From Altoona, Pennsylvania to Zeeland, Michigan, good eats await. The Fire app gives you three main searching methods: plain ol' text entry (use the search monocle), browsing a list of categories, or spinning the famous slot machine wheels. When you launch the app, it asks you to pick which city you're looking in—a choice that you can always change. A recent addition to the Urbanspoon family is Rezbook, available in a few big cities like New York and Los Angeles. It's a reservation system, integrated with the booking software of select restaurants. When it's available, it's a nice way to lock in a table before you head out.

Travel

About to go on the road again? Sure, you're packin' your smartphone, but what a pain that is when it comes to reading through itineraries, brushing up on your tourist trivia, or spotting weather patterns. You've got the Fire's big(ger) screen. Make use of it with these traveler's aids.

- **TripAdvisor (free).** This outfit's website has become one of the most popular sources for hotel, restaurant, and other travel-related info. Composed almost entirely of its members contributions, it's become a kind of Wikipedia for the travel set. On your Fire, the app is more or less a repackaged version of the website. More interesting are a couple dozen city-specific TripAdvisor guides (from Amsterdam and Barcelona to Rome and Washington, DC) that the firm released in late 2011. These are also free and, best of all, work without WiFi. So you can pack your Fire, open it on a park bench, and make spontaneous itinerary changes whenever you feel like it. Each one of these titles is packed with enough tips to send shivers down the spine of a travel guidebook publisher: self-guided tours, neighborhood previews and histories (written by TripAdvisor volunteers), and an "interactive" map, tagged with popular destinations.

- **TripIt (free).** Here's the best way to get Fire to virtually suck down all those random trip logistics (flight info, hotel confirmation, car rental details). What you can track and view with this app is pretty comprehensive. All the usual suspects like flight, hotel, and car info are there, but you can also keep watch on a secondary cast of characters: meeting and expense notes, directions, and even those random activity details ("relish factory tour starts at the pickle stand"). Set up a free account on *www.tripit.com*, and everything gets piped from Web to app. Don't miss some of the service's best, timesaving detail entry tools, like a feature that lets you forward confirmation emails to a special address, which plucks out and records in your account all the key details. The app is capable enough to let you add and adjust plans once you've left your computer. And, of course, it stores all the info on your device (as opposed to pulling it off the Web each time). That way, you don't need WiFi running every time you want to review where you're going next.

- **ConvertPad – Unit Converter (free).** When you're away from home—especially *far* away—figuring out how many dollars you're about to spend or how far, exactly, you're about to walk can be tough. This app is ready to translate from one country's measures to another's. It's got all the common questions covered: length, currency, cooking units, temperature. And it's also prepared to field a few dozen minor measures that will surely appeal to the needs of some traveler at some point (radiation exposure? magnetic flux density? you're covered).

- **AccuWeather (free).** This app's for weather geeks and civilians alike. The basics are here, of course: a home screen with info on current conditions and swipe-to-view additional screens filled with detailed, hourly forecasts. You also get a seven-day forecast, a radar map (including a fun-to-play-with animation depicting recent weather system movement), and practically up-to-the minute video feeds from the company's extensive network of meteorologists, who serve around 175,000 business, government, and other serious-about-weather clients around the world. Add as many favorite locations as you like for the easy one-tap scoop on your most frequent destinations.

Bills and Banking

Keeping tabs on your spending is no vacationer's idea of fun. Options tend to range from blowing it off and hoping you're staying on budget to shoving receipts in an envelope. These apps make on-the-run money tracking much simpler.

- **Mint.com Personal Finance (free).** This popular, free service, run by finance software biggie Intuit, helps you monitor your money. You don't use Mint to pay bills; instead, it pulls in the transaction info from any account you designate (checking, credit cards, loans, investments) and gives you lots of ways to track how you spend your money. Easy to understand pie charts, budgeting tools, and notification alerts (you just spent 187% more this month on tanning than usual) give you a clearer picture of what's going where. A huge timesaver for categorizing expenses is Mint's auto-tagging feature. As it slurps in transactions, it assigns them labels—salary, mortgage, dining, and so on—so you don't have to spend way too much time entering them by hand. If you're not already using the service, you can also get started right on the Fire (but it's easier to sign up on the Web). The app doesn't have all the fine-tuning capabilities and bells and whistles you get on the web version (transaction history lookups for specific merchants, pretty graphs). But you get an on-the-go ledger and helpful budget overviews to keep you honest.

- **PocketMoney ($4.99; Lite version free).** If the power of Mint lies in its everything-stored-online convenience, this app's all about staying *off* the Web. Its main attraction, for many home bookkeepers, is the stop-gap service it provides Quicken and Microsoft Money fans who want their data on the Fire. Until Fire-friendly versions of those tools arrive, this app's a handy way to move transaction data in both directions: from a regular computer (equipped with PocketMoney for Desktops; $19.95) to your Fire, and vice versa. Mind you, Quicken and Money aren't actually required—PocketMoney packs most of their core features (track expenses and income, create budgets, and so on). So if you're looking to ditch those tools, here's one reason to make the switch. Another bonus is the app's syncing talents. You can rig up a partner's Fire, Android phone, or iOS device and funnel everything into one master account. PocketMoney's paid version is ad-free and lets you track as many accounts as you want and do things like track repeating transactions. The free version includes ads and comes without those extras.

- **Office Calculator Pro ($1.69; basic version free).** Who even buys calculators anymore? Engineers, sure. But sometimes even (or perhaps especially) English majors need a hand when it's time to tally a list of figures. This app is simple to use and, weighing in at about 1/4 of a megabyte, occupies just the right amount of space to justify keeping it on your Fire fulltime. It's got a handful of customization options, from cosmetic (button colors) to operational (how many decimal places do you want?). And it's got a nice virtual tape to review calculations post-entry. The free version comes with ads; the paid edition removes the ads and gives you a larger tap area.

Appendixes

APPENDIX A
Settings

APPENDIX B
Troubleshooting and Maintenance

Settings

THE BRIGADE OF HELPERS that drop down when you tap the home screen's Quick Settings icon (Volume, Brightness, WiFi, and the others described on page 22) are usually all you need to adjust your Fire. Sometimes, however, further tweaking is called for. When you've got misbehaving apps or you think you're running out of storage room or power, for example, a trip to the Quick Settings' More button is in order. This Appendix gives you a guided tour through its many options.

Help and Feedback

Three tabs worth of help documents and contact links greet you here: FAQ & Troubleshooting; Contact Customer Service; and Feedback. Use the second and third tabs to reach an Amazon rep and submit questions and comments about the Fire. The first tab lists about two dozen support topics, ranging from "Home Screen and Navigation" to "Connecting to Wi-Fi." Is there anything here that you *won't* find in the preceding pages of this book? Probably not—it's just a copy of what you'll find online at *http://amzn.to/kfmm155*. Nothing wrong with any of that, of course, but don't expect to find advice on real-world workarounds or commentary on what's worth your time and what's still a work-in-progress. To be fair, though, Amazon does win one round in this particular help-off: It can update these help files in a way that's not possible with a published book. As Amazon adds new features to the Fire, you can expect to find some basic coverage in these online help guides.

My Account

Two items of note in this section. The dedicated email address is where you send Word and PDF files you want to read on your Fire (page 76). The Deregister button is how you uncouple a Fire from your Amazon account. You may want to do that if you give away or sell the gadget to someone else. That way, the new owner sees the digital items he buys from Amazon on his new (that is, used) Fire.

Restrictions

Page 24 has the full scoop about how to activate this lock. In essence, it's a WiFi network barrier that's helpful for parents who want to keep kids from wandering online when using the Fire.

Sounds

A volume slider lets you control sound level—though you can get to the same control much faster by tapping the Quick Settings icon (page 22) on the home screen. In the Notifications Sounds menu, choose from any of the two dozen or so engagingly named options—Caffeinated Rattlesnake, Don't Panic, Missed It—to control the noise your Fire emits when an app wants to notify you that something's just happened (a newly arrived email or tweet, for example).

Display

As with the volume control, this item is a longer alternate route to the Quick Setting's brightness slider. Below it, Screen Timeout lists eight options—ranging from 30 seconds to Never. Choose one of these to control how quickly your Fire falls asleep (page 19) if you don't touch it. The longer the screen remains lit, of course, the quicker your battery drains.

Security

Turn the Lock Screen Password on if you'd like anyone who uses your Fire—including, of course, yourself—to enter a code before being allowed onto the home screen. The password prompt appears after you swipe the lock screen's orange arrow. Page 24 explains how to install this particular lock. The next two options—Credential Storage and Device Administrators—are for those who want to join highly secured WiFi networks (ask your friendly IT person for what to enter to join a VPN network) and for third-party apps like the Exchange-friendly Touchdown (see the Note on page 149) that require a special password to control some under-the-hood functions of the Fire.

Applications

Anyone who's familiar with Windows' Task Manager will get the gist of this section.

Every app on the Fire gets its own page here, filled with a common set of controls for doing administrative things like force quitting, uninstalling the app, or flushing out its contents (all the contacts in the Address Book app, for example). The "Filter by" menu at the top of the page gives you three options to adjust the number of apps that appear on this screen: Running Applications lists only the open apps; Third Party Applications shows you any apps not installed on the Fire when you first turned it on; and All Applications shows every app currently on your device. If you've installed any apps from the Appstore—Angry Birds, IMDb, Netflix—you'll see 'em here. (Apps you've purchased but haven't yet downloaded to the Fire don't appear on any of these lists.) Every app comes with a dedicated page that almost always includes the following sections:

- **App name.** Aside from its official name, you find the app's version number (the version you currently have installed, that is). Two buttons—Force Stop and Uninstall—let you do just what you'd expect.

- **Storage.** Here you can check how much memory the app and its associated contents are taking up (the latter is reflected in the line that says "Data"). Tap the Clear Data button to keep the app on your Fire but empty out any files, contact listings, to do lists, and so on.

- **Cache.** Apps use this temporary memory storage bin to access frequently needed info or recently visited content. The Silk web browser, for example, keeps its History list (page 176) stored here. Tap "Clear Cache" to empty this receptacle.

- **Launch by default.** Some tasks on the Fire require the help of an app—opening a picture, for example, can be done with the built-in Gallery app or any third-party app that's image friendly. Here's where you can *unpick* an app that's currently selected as the chosen helper. Next time the Fire needs help showing a picture (attached to an email, say), you can then pick from a list of available choices.

- **Permissions.** The list shown here details everything an app can—or can't—do with your Fire. Typical entries include things like "modify/delete Internal storage contents," which simply means that the app can save or change files. That's useful for any of the Office apps detailed in Chapter 5. The information is strictly read-only. In other words, you can't actually prevent an app from performing any of the actions listed here.

NOTE If you poke around these lists and see some apps with oddly familiar names, recall that pretty much every feature on your Fire—the search oval, the Status bar, the Music Library—is its own app. In other words, the apps named Search, Status Bar, and Amazon MP3, respectively, control each of those three functions. You never have to actually launch apps with those names; instead, they automatically kick in every time you turn on the Fire.

Date and Time

Turn the first option—Automatic—to On to have an online master timekeeper set the correct date and time on your Fire. Even if you occasionally go offline (for a car trip, say), the Fire's internal ticker keeps things on track. You'll also want to pick whatever region you're in from the last option—Select Time Zone. If you want to adjust these settings manually, turn Automatic Off and then adjust the time and date to your liking using the Set Time and Set Date options.

Wireless Network

Here's WiFi central. Everything you learned how to do back in Chapter 1—select a network to log onto, enter a password, add a network—you can do here. Here's also where you can turn WiFi off entirely, using the On/Off switch at the top of the screen.

Kindle Keyboard

The three options here let you customize how things work when it's time to type. Turn on "Sound on keypress" to get a tinny, clicking noise each time you hit a key. Do the same with "Auto-capitalization," and every time you type a period, the next letter you enter is automatically capitalized. Finally, "Quick fixes" is the Fire's version of Microsoft Word's auto-correct feature. You can't customize this one, however; your choices are simply On or Off.

Device

This section has a long list of read-only status reports on the state of your Fire. The first two items—Application Storage and Internal Storage—tally how much memory you've used up, and how much remains. Battery charge remaining comes next, followed by items showing the version number of your Fire's system software and the device's serial number. Next up: Your WiFi MAC Address, which a network administrator may ask you for in order to let you on some company's WiFi network. Turn "Allow Installation of Applications" on only if you're following the hacker's tutorial pointed out in the Note on page 30. And tap the final item—Reset to Factory Defaults—only if you'd like to wipe your Fire clean and start from scratch. Tapping this option gets you a pop-up box containing two buttons: "Erase everything" and the *no, thanks, I changed my mind* Cancel button.

Legal Notices

A message from the lawyers, part one, in which Amazon lists all the patent, trademark, and copyright muscle protecting the Fire. Here's also where Amazon gives a shout out to all the open source and other software it used to make this particular Kindle sparkle.

Terms of Use

Message from the lawyers, part two, in which you're taken to a web page with links to a dozen or so highly detailed documents. Each describes what you can—or cannot—do when using the Amazon MP3 music service, the Amazon Appstore, Amazon Prime, and so on.

Troubleshooting and Maintenance

IT'S HAPPENED ON EVERY electronic device ever invented and it's probably going to happen to your Fire: the screen freezes up, a download gets stuck in mid-descent, something stops responding. The fixes come in two basic flavors—what's easy and what's obvious. That's because, unlike a regular computer, there's not much fiddling a non-engineer can do on the Fire. Maneuvers like a simple restart, a hard reset, and software updates usually will solve most problems.

When you stumble upon one of the half dozen or so typical glitches covered in this appendix, one of the following two remedies usually gets your Fire back on track:

- **Restart.** Sounds simple, sure, but this procedure solves a heck of a lot of Fire's problems. Start by pressing the bottom edge's power button for a second or so (definitely longer than a quick tap, which only puts the Fire to sleep). When the Fire asks *Do you want to shut down your Kindle?*, tap Shut Down. Wait about 15 seconds after the screen goes dark and then power back up by pressing, briefly, the same button.

- **Hard reset.** The equivalent of pressing Ctrl-Alt-Delete on Windows or holding the power button down on the Mac, you're instructing the Fire to flush its short-term digital memory and reboot. To make it so, press and hold the Fire's power button for 20 seconds; the screen will go completely black and the Fire shuts down. Now restart the device by pressing the power button (briefly, not longer than a second). It will perform a normal startup sequence and bring you back to the regular welcome point, the lock screen.

> **TIP** Seeing a pop-up menu or anything onscreen (a dialog box, message window, and so on) that's keeping you from reaching the underlying app's main screen? Try tapping the Back button on the Options bar (see the Note on page 23).

WiFi Not Working

The most common symptom strikes when you're waking the Fire up. You press the power button, swipe open the lock screen, and then launch an app. Up pops the telltale "No Internet Connection" message box. On the Status bar's right edge, check to see if the WiFi icon is on (one to four curved white bars, with more bars equaling a stronger connection). Often as not, the Fire just needs a few more seconds—sometimes as many as 10—to reacquaint itself with the WiFi network after waking up. If, after waiting, you're still not getting online, try turning the Fire's WiFi off and then back on (in the Quick Settings drop-down menu, tap WiFi and then Off; wait a minute, then repeat and flip the switch back on). A tiny "x" on the bottom row of the WiFi icon means you've got a link with the WiFi network, but it's not yet letting you on the Internet. The most common reason: You're at a restaurant, hotel, or airport and the network wants you to register or pay before passing go. Follow the instructions in the box on page 101 to do so.

> **TIP** Want to forget a network that the Fire keeps connecting to? On the Quick Setting's WiFi list, tap and hold any network name. From the dialog box that pops up, tap Forget.

Unresponsive App

Before turning to the restart or hard reset, one fix worth trying out is buried in the Quick Settings→More→Applications section. As you learned in the previous Appendix (page 243), here's where the control panel for each app resides. Find the app that's giving you grief (if necessary, in the "Filter by" menu at the top of the screen, pick All Applications), tap its name, and at the top of the screen, press Force Stop. A message box asks if you're sure you want to do so; tap OK and then reopen the app back on the Fire's main screen.

App Installation Problems

The typical sequence you see when downloading an app is to watch the button showing its price (or, in the case of giveaways, "Free") cycle through the following labels: Purchasing, Downloading, Installing, and Open. Sometimes things get stuck on the Installing phase. More often than not the app has actually finished its installation. The fix? Ye olde restart, as outlined on page 247. You should then see the new app listed in the Device section of your Apps library.

Out-of-Date Apps

The word "apps" is just another word for "software." And as with the software on a regular computer, the manufacturers often issue updates. One of the best parts about owning a Fire, and using its apps, is you don't have to keep track of where to get these improvements and bug fixes, nor do you have to figure out when they're available. All you have to do is glance at the Notifications circle (up on the left edge of the Status bar). Whenever a new edition of any app is available, a number appears in this circle. Tap it, and under the Update Available tab you'll see a list of whichever apps have new versions waiting.

System Software Updates

For the first year or so of the Fire's life, you can expect Amazon to periodically release new versions of the operating software (the Fire's equivalent of Windows 7 or Mac OS X Lion). Normally these updates get installed automatically, downloading as soon as they're available and your Fire is connected to a WiFi network. Your work in that case is pretty minimal: Turn the Fire on, watch the onscreen message inform you of a system update in progress, after which the Fire shuts down and restarts itself. (If the Fire is asleep and connected to WiFi, this entire process may take place without you even noticing.) In any case, if you learn via the Web that a new update is available and can't wait for it to roll your way, tap Quick Settings→Sync. The update will download automatically.

> **NOTE** These software updates can be hefty, weighing in at 200 MB or more. If you've got a speedy wired Internet connection (at work, say), you can download the update to a computer and then sideload it to the Fire, after connecting the two machines via a USB cable (page 77). Follow the instructions here—*http://amzn.to/kfmm147*—for full details.

Battery Draining Too Quickly

If your battery seems to deliver less than Amazon's predicted seven to eight hours of steady use, WiFi may be the culprit. If you're not getting a strong signal, the Fire may be working extra hard to stay connected. To check your signal strength, go to Quick Settings→Wi-Fi and see how many curved bars are emboldened on the network labeled Connected. More is better; if you're only getting one or two, that may be the problem. If practical, move your Fire closer to your WiFi router for a stronger connection. Another option: Before going to sleep, turn WiFi off (on the same screen, above the network list, flip the On switch to Off).

Sharing or Selling Your Fire

Ready to hand over your Fire to someone else? Whether you're selling it on eBay or giving it to a relative, your best bet is to wipe it clean. That's not just for security's sake. Even if you're giving it to someone you trust, you want them to be able to hook the device into their own Amazon account (page 17) so that their ebooks, music, and so on show up when they power up. To wipe things clean, head to Quick Settings→Device and pick the final item on the list: Reset to Factory Defaults. You'll need to confirm that you really want to do this (tap "Erase everything" on the pop-up box that appears), and then you've got a good-as-new Fire to hand over.

Where to Head for Help

A few helpful troubleshooting websites have popped up since the Fire's initial release.

- **Amazon's Fire Support page** (*http://amzn.to/kfmm149*). Amazon's official online help desk. Nothing here qualifies as an undocumented tip or trick, but it's a useful site to bookmark for basic troubleshooting.

- **Amazon's Kindle discussion forums** (*http://amzn.to/kfmm157*). This section of the retailer's site is loaded with active, opinionated, and often very helpful conversations. Use the search box on the lower right (Search Customer Discussions) to home in on specific topics.

- **Android Forums.** This geeky site has a lively section devoted to the Fire (*http://bit.ly/kfmm151*). Advice seeker beware: Plenty of answers on here are home-grown and by no means street legal (or, for that matter, safe). But you will find a lot of step-by-step instructions and responsive, if not especially patient, feedback on almost anything you'd want to do with the Fire.

- **XDA Developers.** Similar to the previous site, but geared slightly more to app developers. Still, the site has a highly trafficked and more or less consumer-oriented discussion area devoted to the Fire: *http://bit.ly/kfmm153*.

Index